American Language Hub

STARTER B
Student's Book

INGRID WISNIEWSKA
ED PRICE

macmillan education

Contents

	LESSON • OBJECTIVES	GRAMMAR	VOCABULARY	PRONUNCIATION	READING • LISTENING	SPEAKING • WRITING
U7	**SKILLS**					
7.1	**What can you do?** (p50) Talk about your abilities	***can/can't***	abilities	*can/can't*: /æ/ and /ə/	read an article about animals vs humans	conduct a class survey about abilities
7.2	**He's amazing!** (p52) Talk about people's talents	**possessive *'s***	adjectives	possessive *'s*	listen to a radio show about a very talented family **KEY SKILL** Listening for pronoun reference	**SPEAKING HUB** ask and answer questions to find out about a talented person
7.3	**Café Hub** **New hair** (p54) Make polite requests		book an appointment		watch someone book an appointment on the phone	
	UNIT REVIEW (p56)	**WRITING** (p56) Write a competition entry | **KEY SKILL** Using commas in lists				
U8	**THE HERE AND NOW**					
8.1	**What's he doing?** (p58) Describe what people are doing	**present progressive**	verb phrases	different ways to pronounce *a*	listen to a conversation between police officers	describe a picture and find the differences
8.2	**The gray coat** (p60) Talk about clothes	**adjective order**	clothes	vowel sounds: /iː/, /ɜː/, /uː/ and /ɔː/	read a text message exchange between friends **KEY SKILL** Identifying key words	**SPEAKING HUB** talk about clothes in different situations
8.3	**Café Hub** **Too loud** (p62) Shop for clothes		shop for clothes		watch someone buy something for a friend	
	UNIT REVIEW (p64)	**WRITING** (p64) Write a short message | **KEY SKILL** Using *also* and *too*				
U9	**LOOKING BACK**					
9.1	**Famous faces** (p66) Talk about famous people from the past	**simple past: *was/were***	dates and years	*was he / was she*	listen to a guide about famous people's lives	ask and answer questions about a famous person
9.2	**Voices from the past** (p68) Talk about people's achievements	**simple past: regular verbs**	everyday verbs	past tense endings: /d/, /t/ and /ɪd/	read a text about a new children's book **KEY SKILL** Scanning	**SPEAKING HUB** complete a quiz about famous people
9.3	**Café Hub** **Pizza Roma** (p70) Make recommendations		ask for and give recommendations		watch someone ask for restaurant recommendations	
	UNIT REVIEW (p72)	**WRITING** (p72) Write a short biography | **KEY SKILL** Organizing your notes				

	LESSON • OBJECTIVES	GRAMMAR	VOCABULARY	PRONUNCIATION	READING • LISTENING	SPEAKING • WRITING
U10	**IT'S HISTORY**					
10.1	**Precious finds** (p74) Talk about past events	**simple past: irregular verbs**	time phrases	vowel sounds: /ɔː/ and /oʊ/	read *A history of the world in 100 objects*	choose 5 objects to represent the world today
10.2	**Family treasures** (p76) Talk about past experiences	**simple past questions**	life events	final consonant /t/ and /d/	listen to a podcast where people talk about treasured objects **KEY SKILL** Identifying reasons	**SPEAKING HUB** conduct a survey to find out about people's past experiences
10.3	**Café Hub** **It was amazing!** (p78) Talk about what you did on the weekend		show interest		▶ watch people discuss what they did on the weekend	
	UNIT REVIEW (p80)	**WRITING** (p80) Write a paragraph about a past event | **KEY SKILL** Using sequencing words				
U11	**HAVING FUN**					
11.1	**In or out?** (p82) Talk about things you like doing	***like/love/hate/ enjoy* + verb + *-ing***	recreational activities	verb + *-ing* /ŋ/	read a lifestyle article about staying in or going out	discuss what you like doing in your free time
11.2	**Super fans** (p84) Talk about favorite sports, music and movies	**object pronouns**	entertainment	vowel sounds: /ʊ/ and /uː/	listen to a radio show interview with fans **KEY SKILL** Listening for opinions	**SPEAKING HUB** ask and answer questions to find a super fan
11.3	**Café Hub** **Short run** (p86) Make and respond to suggestions		make and respond to suggestions		▶ watch someone make plans to see a friend	
	UNIT REVIEW (p88)	**WRITING** (p88) Write a personal profile | **KEY SKILL** Using *so*				
U12	**GOING AWAY**					
12.1	**Trips** (p90) Describe a trip	**countable and uncountable nouns**	travel	consonant clusters	read about trips that go wrong	talk about a bad trip you went on
12.2	**A prize vacation** (p92) Talk about vacation plans	**present progressive**	types of vacations	vowel sounds: /ɪ/, /iː/ and /aɪ/	listen to a competition winner on the radio **KEY SKILL** Listening for feelings	**SPEAKING HUB** Discuss and plan your dream vacation
12.3	**Café Hub** **Istanbul** (p94) Ask for and give opinions		ask for and give opinions		▶ watch two friends talk about vacation destinations	
	UNIT REVIEW (p96)	**WRITING** (p96) Write a postcard | **KEY SKILL** Editing your writing				

Irregular Verbs (pIV) **Grammar Hub** (pVI) **Vocabulary Hub** (pXXVIII) **Communication Hub** (pXXI) **Audio scripts** (pXXIV)

Irregular Verbs

Base form	Simple past	Past participle
be	was/were	been
become	became	become
begin	began	begun
break	broke	broken
bring	brought	brought
build	built	built
buy	bought	bought
can	could	(been able to)
catch	caught	caught
choose	chose	chosen
come	came	come
cost	cost	cost
cut	cut	cut
do	did	done
drink	drank	drunk
eat	ate	eaten
fall	fell	fallen
feel	felt	felt
find	found	found
forget	forgot	forgotten
get	got	got
give	gave	given
go	went	gone/been
grow	grew	grown
have	had	had
hear	heard	heard
hit	hit	hit
hold	held	held
hurt	hurt	hurt
keep	kept	kept
know	knew	known
leave	left	left
lend	lent	lent

Base form	Simple past	Past participle
let	let	let
lose	lost	lost
make	made	made
mean	meant	meant
meet	met	met
must	had to	(had to)
pay	paid	paid
put	put	put
read	read	read
ride	rode	ridden
run	ran	run
say	said	said
see	saw	seen
sell	sold	sold
set	set	set
shut	shut	shut
sing	sang	sung
sit	sat	sat
sleep	slept	slept
speak	spoke	spoken
spell	spelled	spelled
spend	spent	spent
stand	stood	stood
steal	stole	stolen
take	took	taken
teach	taught	taught
tell	told	told
think	thought	thought
throw	threw	thrown
understand	understood	understood
wear	wore	worn
win	won	won
write	wrote	written

PHONETIC SYMBOLS											
Single vowels			Diphthongs			Consonants					
/ɪ/	fish	/fɪʃ/	/uw/	new	/nuw/	/p/	pen	/pen/	/s/	snake	/sneɪk/
/iː/	bean	/biːn/	/eɪ/	face	/feɪs/	/b/	bag	/bæg/	/z/	zoo	/zuː/
/ʊ/	foot	/fʊt/	/ɔɪ/	boy	/bɔɪ/	/t/	tea	/tiː/	/ʃ/	shop	/ʃɒp/
/uː/	shoe	/ʃuː/	/oʊ/	nose	/noʊz/	/d/	dog	/dɒg/	/ʒ/	television	/'telɪvɪʒən/
/e/	egg	/eg/	/ju/	use	/juz/	/ʧ/	chip	/ʧɪp/	/m/	map	/mæp/
/ə/	mother	/'mʌðər/	/aɪ/	eye	/aɪ/	/ʤ/	jazz	/ʤæz/	/n/	name	/neɪm/
/ɜː/	word	/wɜːrd/	/aʊ/	mouth	/maʊθ/	/k/	cake	/keɪk/	/ŋ/	ring	/rɪŋ/
/ɔː/	talk	/tɔːk/				/g/	girl	/gɜːrl/	/h/	house	/haʊs/
/æ/	back	/bæk/				/f/	film	/fɪlm/	/l/	leg	/leg/
/ʌ/	bus	/bʌs/				/v/	verb	/vɜːrb/	/r/	road	/roʊd/
/ɑː/	arm	/ɑːrm/				/θ/	thing	/θɪŋ/	/w/	want	/wɒnt/
/ɒ/	top	/tɒp/				/ð/	these	/ðiːz/	/j/	yes	/jes/

7 SKILLS

> If you think you can do it, you can.
>
> John Burroughs

Performer with the Chinese State Circus, London, England.

OBJECTIVES

- talk about your abilities
- talk about people's talents
- make polite requests
- write a competition entry

Work with a partner. Discuss the questions.

1 Look at the picture. What can you see?

2 Look at the picture again. Choose the correct options to complete the description.

There is a [1]*man* / *woman*. He has a lot of things on his [2]*head* / *hand*. He has [3]*black* / *gray* hair. There's a [4]*bag* / *bird* at the top.

3 Read the quote. Do you agree?

7.1 What can you do?

Talk about your abilities

G *can/can't* **P** *can/can't*: /æ/ and /ə/ **V** abilities

READING

A PREPARE TO READ Work in pairs. Look at the pictures (a–c) in the article and discuss the questions.

1 What can you see in the pictures?
2 What sport do you think each picture shows?

B READ FOR MAIN IDEA Read the article quickly. Choose the correct options.

1 This article is about what some …
  a animals can't do. b people can do.
2 This writer talks to three people about …
  a their abilities. b their pets.
3 The people can do …
  a amazing things. b useful things.

C READ FOR KEY INFORMATION Read the article again. Choose the correct numbers to complete the sentences.

2 4 (x2) 6 80 500

1 Luis can climb ______________ meters up a mountain in ______________ hours.
2 Seon-Yeong can fly for ______________ kilometers. She can be in the air for ______________ minutes.
3 Ireen can swim down ______________ meters. She can be underwater for ______________ minutes.

D READ FOR DETAIL Read the article again. Are the statements true (T) or false (F)?

1 Animals and humans have some of the same skills. *T / F*
2 Free climbing is very dangerous. *T / F*
3 Wingsuit flyers needs to take off from a high place. *T / F*
4 Free divers don't take any extra air when they go underwater. *T / F*

E SPEAK Work in groups. Answer the questions

1 Which sport in the text do you want to try?
2 Are there other sports you want to try?

I want to try wingsuit flying – it looks really fun!

GRAMMAR

can/can't

A WORK IT OUT Read the examples from the article. Choose the correct option to complete the rule.

Animals can do many things that humans can't do.
A: Can you really fly?
B: Yes, I can!

can/can't
We use *can/can't* to talk about ***abilities*** / ***routines***.

B WORK IT OUT Read the examples again. Choose the correct options to complete the rules.

can/can't
1 After *can* and *can't* we use a **verb with** ***to*** / **verb without** ***to***. We always use the same form of the verb with all subjects.
2 We **use** / **don't use** *do* and *don't* in questions and negative sentences with *can/can't*.

C Go to the **Grammar Hub** on **page VI**.

ANIMALS VS HUMANS

As we all know, animals can do many things that humans can't do. Birds can fly, fish can swim and breathe underwater, and monkeys can climb. Humans can't. Or can we? This week we talk to three amazing humans about their abilities.

Interviewer: Luis, what exactly is a free climber?

A free climber doesn't use ropes to help them climb, only to stop them from falling. Sometimes it's a little bit dangerous. I can't climb for very long because it's difficult and I get tired. I can climb about 500 meters in four hours.

Interviewer: Seon-Yeong, can you really fly?

Yes, I can! I'm a wingsuit flyer in my free time. Birds take off from the ground, but I can't. I jump from somewhere really high, like the top of a mountain or from a plane. I can fly for about four kilometers, and I'm usually in the air for two minutes.

Interviewer: Ireen, you're a free diver – how long can you stay underwater?

I can hold my breath for about six minutes. I don't have an air tank, so I am very careful when I dive. I can dive about 80 meters down and then I need to come up again. I love it, it's so quiet underwater!

a

b

c

D PRACTICE Order the words to make questions and answers.

1 A: you / swim / can

____?

B: can / yes, / I

____.

2 A: a monkey / fly / can

____?

B: no, / can't / it

____.

3 A: you / can / what / do

____?

B: can / a mountain / I / climb

____.

4 A: which / can / live / animal / underwater

____?

B: live / can / underwater / a fish

____.

PRONUNCIATION

can/can't: /æ/ and /ə/

7.1 **A** Listen and repeat the sounds, words and examples.

/æ/ can	**A:** Can you climb? **B:** Yes, I can.
/ə/ can	**A:** What can you do? **B:** I can swim.
/æ/ can't	I can't fly.

B SPEAK Work in pairs. Ask questions like the ones in Exercise A. Give answers that are true for you.

A: Can you climb?

B: Yes, I can. I can't climb a mountain. I can climb a tree! What can you do?

VOCABULARY

Abilities

A Complete the sentences with the verbs in the box.

cook dance draw juggle sing ski

1 Helia can ____________.

4 Pablo can ____________.

2 Gus can ____________.

5 Mira can ____________.

3 Gina can ____________.

6 Alex can ____________.

B Match the verbs (1–6) to the nouns (a–f) to make phrases.

1 drive ___	3 do ___	5 ride ___
2 play ___	4 paint ___	6 speak ___
a French	c the guitar	e a car
b yoga	d a picture	f a motorcycle

C Write the correct phrases from Exercise B under each picture.

a 

____

b 

____

c 

____

d 

____

e 

____

f 

____

D Go to the **Vocabulary Hub** on **page XVIII**.

SPEAKING

A PREPARE You are going to interview your classmates. Work in pairs. Choose five abilities from the ideas below or use your own ideas.

ride a motorcycle draw climb a mountain swim juggle ski play the piano speak Spanish dance cook drive a car

B PLAN Write one question about each ability you chose.

Can you ride a motorcycle?

C PRACTICE Go around the class. Find people who can do each activity on your list.

A: Can you ride a motorcycle?

B: Yes, I can.

D REPORT Work in groups. Tell the group the results of your survey.

A: Three people can ride a motorcycle.

B: Six people can draw.

Talk about your abilities

7.2 He's amazing!

Talk about people's talents

S listening for pronoun reference V adjectives G possessive *'s* P possessive *'s*

Sheku Kanneh-Mason

LISTENING

A PREPARE TO LISTEN Look at the picture. Choose the correct words to complete the sentences. There are three words you don't need.

cellos dancers guitars musicians pianos violins

1 These people are ______________.
2 Two people have ______________.
3 Three people have ______________.

7.2 **B LISTEN FOR GIST** Listen to a radio show. Find and correct three mistakes in the summary.

Sheku Kanneh-Mason is a musician. He has eight brothers and sisters. They all study at the Royal Academy of Music. Their parents play musical instruments.

Listening for pronoun reference

We use pronouns (*I, you, we, they, he, she, it, this, that*) and adverbs (*there, here*) so we don't need to repeat names of people and places. Listen for a name or a place and think about the pronoun or adverb the speaker will use in their next sentence.

Sheku Kanneh-Mason*'s an amazing musician.* ***He****'s the winner of the 2016 BBC Young Musician of the Year Award.*

Oliver: Are they students at the ***Royal Academy of Music****, as well?*

Carrie: No, they don't go ***there*** *– not yet anyway.*

7.2 **C LISTEN FOR DETAIL** Listen again. Match the names of people and places (1–6) with their connection to Sheku (a–f).

1 Braimah
2 Isata
3 Kadiatu and Stuart
4 Nottingham
5 Royal Academy of Music

a his parents
b his sister
c his brother
d where he lives
e where he studies

D SPEAK Work in pairs. Answer the questions.

1 Can you play a musical instrument? Which one(s)?
2 Who is talented in your family? What can they do?

VOCABULARY

Adjectives

A Read the sentences from the radio show. The underlined word in sentence 1 is an adjective. Underline the adjectives in sentences 2 and 3.

1 *Every day we talk about an interesting person.*
2 *Today's person is a young musician.*
3 *It's difficult to find the time to play an instrument …*

B Match the adjectives in Exercise A with their definitions.

1 Someone who is ______________ has lived for only a short time.
2 Something that is ______________ is not easy to do or understand.
3 Something, or someone, that is ______________ is exciting and unusual.

C Read the sentences in Exercise A again. Choose the correct option to complete the rules.

1 We use adjectives ***before*** / ***after*** a noun.
2 We use adjectives on their own ***before*** / ***after*** the verb *be*.

D Underline the adjectives in these sentences.

1 He's an amazing musician.
2 My sisters are all great swimmers.
3 Fionn and Carla are both bad dancers.
4 Lois's singing is terrible.
5 Oliver's a talented artist.
6 Juan's dad is awful at cooking.
7 This is a boring book.
8 I eat a lot of healthy food.

E Work in pairs. Complete the table with the adjectives in Exercise D. Are they positive (+) or negative (–)?

Positive	Negative
amazing	

F SPEAK Use the adjectives in the box to complete the sentences so they are true for you. Tell your partner.

amazing bad boring difficult easy good OK talented terrible

1 I'm a(n) ______________ musician.
2 I think it's ______________ to play the cello.
3 I think it's ______________ to have a big family.
4 I think music with violins and cellos is ______________.

GRAMMAR
Possessive 's

A Read the sentences from the radio show. Underline the words with the possessive 's.

1 Braimah is Sheku's brother.
2 Sheku's parents' names are Kadiatu and Stuart.

B **WORK IT OUT** Choose the correct option to complete the rule.

We use 's and ' to say that someone or something *belongs to* / *happens to* someone or something.

C **WORK IT OUT** Read the sentences again. Add 's or ' to complete the rules and examples.

Possessive 's

We use [1]____ after singular nouns: *Sheku is Braimah* [2]____ *brother.*
We use [3]____ after plural nouns ending in -s: *His sisters* [4]____ *names are Isata, Konya, Jeneba, Aminatu and Mariatu.*

D **PRACTICE** Add 's or ' in the correct place to complete the sentences.

1 My mother name is Kali. *My mother's name is Kali.*
2 Luke favorite instrument is the violin.
3 My two cousins house is in the city.
4 Alice's parents names are Olive and Oscar.
5 All of the musicians instruments are in the next room.
6 Alberto is Carlos brother.

E **WORK IT OUT** Read the information and choose the correct options.

Possessive 's, *is* and *has*

We also use 's as a short form of *is* or *has*.
His name's Sheku Kanneh-Mason. (= his name [1]*is* / *has*)
He's done his homework. (= he [2]*is* / *has*)

F **PRACTICE** Choose the correct meaning of 's in these sentences.

1 Mark's my father. *is* / *has* / *possessive 's*
2 My father's name is Mark. *is* / *has* / *possessive 's*
3 Mark's gone to the store. *is* / *has* / *possessive 's*

G Go to the **Grammar Hub** on **page VI**.

H **SPEAK** Work in pairs. Tell your partner about the following things …

• your family • your home • your hobby

My sister is a musician. My home is in Costa Rica. My hobby is swimming.

I **SPEAK** Work in groups. Tell them about your partner. Use possessive 's.

Erica's sister is a musician. Erica's home is in Costa Rica. Erica's hobby is swimming.

PRONUNCIATION
Possessive 's

A 7.3 Listen to how we say the *s* at the end of each of the names in the table.

/z/	/s/	/ɪz/
Aminata's	Albert's	Angus's
______	______	______

B 7.4 Listen to three more names. Write them in the table.

Alex's Anna's Juliet's

C 7.5 Choose the correct pronunciation for the possessive 's at the end of the names. Listen, check and repeat.

1 Marcus's /z/ /s/ /ɪz/
2 Tom's /z/ /s/ /ɪz/
3 Junko's /z/ /s/ /ɪz/
4 Carlos's /z/ /s/ /ɪz/
5 Bec's /z/ /s/ /ɪz/
6 Max's /z/ /s/ /ɪz/

SPEAKING HUB

A Work in pairs. Student A – Stay on this page. Student B – Go to the **Communication Hub** on **page XXIII**.

B **PREPARE** Read the information about this person. Write questions to find the missing information.

HIFUMI ABE is from [1]__________. He is good at judo. He is a world champion. His sister's name is [2]__________. She is good at judo, too. [3]__________ is the 2017 Junior World Champion. They are the winners of the 2017 Tokyo Grand Slam.

1 Where is Hifumi from? 2 What …? 3 Who …?

C **DISCUSS** Work in pairs. Ask your partner questions to complete the missing information. Answer your partner's questions.

D **REPEAT** Repeat with the information below.

JONATHAN BROWNLEE is from England. He is good at [1]__________. He can swim, ride a bicycle and run – and he's fast! His brother is good at [2]__________. His brother's name is Alistair. They both have [3]__________.

E **REFLECT** Think of another amazing person. Tell your partner about them.

Talk about people's talents

Café Hub

7.3 New hair

F– make polite requests

COMPREHENSION

A ▶ 00.54–02:41 **Watch the first part of the video and answer the questions.**

1 Who is Lisa?
2 What sort of hairstyle does Gaby want?
3 What do you think Gaby's new hairstyle is like?

B ▶ 02:42–02:57 **Watch the end of the video. What is Gaby's new hairstyle? Do you like it?**

C **When Gaby says *Wow!* what does she mean?**

1 I love it.
2 I hate it.
3 It's OK.

D **Complete the sentences with the words in the box.**

concert hairstyle Lisa's Hair magazine Spain three o'clock

a Gaby arrives at the hairdresser's at __________.
b Lucy invites Gaby to a friend's __________.
c Gaby calls __________.
d The hairdresser loves __________.
e Gaby wants to change her __________.
f Gaby reads a __________.

E ▶ **Put the events (a–f) in Exercise D in the correct order (1–6). Then watch the video again and check your answers.**

FUNCTIONAL LANGUAGE

Making polite requests

A **Underline the polite phrases. Who said it?**

1 So, Gaby what *do you want* / *would you like*?
a Gaby b Lisa
2 *I'd like* / *I want* something different, please.
a Gaby b Lisa

B **Complete the phrases by putting the word in parentheses in the correct place.**

1 Three o'clock is fine. Can I *have* your phone number, please? (have)
2 I'd like book an appointment, please. (to)
3 Is Lisa's Hair? (that)
4 you have time today? (Do)
5 Yes, is. (it)
6 Yes, today's good. What time would you to come? (like)
7 Yeah sure! When you like to come? (would)

GABY

SAM

LUCY

C Complete the conversation with the phrases from Exercise B.

1 *Is that Lisa's Hair?*

Yes, 2 ______.

3 ______

4 ______

5 ______

6 ______

7 *Three o'clock?*

8 ______

Sure.

D ▶ 01:01–02:05 Watch part of the video again and check your answers to Exercises B and C.

PRONUNCIATION

7.6 **A** Listen to the conversation and notice how the intonation goes up (↗) or goes down (↘) in questions.

Ben: Is this Dr. Jones? (↗)
Dr. Jones: Yes, it is.
Ben: Can I book an appointment, please? (↗)
Dr. Jones: Sure. When would you like to come? (↘)
Ben: Do you have time today? (↗)
Dr. Jones: Yes, today's good. What time? (↘)
Ben: Is two o'clock OK? (↗)
Dr. Jones: Two o'clock's fine. Can I have your phone number, please? (↗)

7.6 **B** Listen again and repeat the conversation. Copy the intonation.

SPEAKING

A PREPARE Work in pairs. Replace the red words in Pronunciation Exercise A with different people, times and places. Use the ideas below or your own ideas. Practice the dialogue.

Person	Day	Time
Dr. Smith	tomorrow	noon
Johanna Mendelsohn, mechanic	Monday	two thirty
Mr. Roberts, bank manager	next Tuesday	four o'clock

B PLAN Make appointments with other students in the class. Put a check mark (✓) next to the six times when you are free today and tomorrow.

	TODAY	TOMORROW
09:00		
10:00		
11:00		
12:00		
1:00		
2:00		
3:00		
4:00		
5:00		
6:00		
7:00		
8:00		

C PRACTICE Go around the class and make appointments with other students. Then change roles and do the activity again.

A: Is this (name of person)?
B: Yes, it is.
A: Can I book an appointment, please?
B: Yes. When would you like to come?
A: Is today at 11 o'clock OK?
B: Sorry, I'm not free. Is 12 o'clock OK?
A: 12 o'clock's fine.

Make polite requests

7 Writing

Write a competition entry

W – using commas in lists

A Read the two texts. Then choose the correct option to complete the sentence.

The texts are applications for a *talent competition* / *sports competition*.

B Work in pairs. Complete the applications with the words in the box.

artist cello dance person picture Spanish

Anyone Can Do It!

Name: Imelda Suarez **Age:** 29

About you: I'm Imelda and I'm from Spain. I love music and I can play the guitar, the piano and the [1] ____________. I can also sing and [2] ____________. I also love languages and I can speak [3] ____________, Italian and English.

Anyone Can Do It!

Name: Lucas Johnson **Age:** 32

About you: I'm Canadian, but I live in Mexico. I really love art. I'm a(n) [4] ____________, and I'm really fast! I can draw, and I can paint a(n) [5] ____________ of any animal, [6] ____________ or thing, and I can do it in one or two minutes!

Using commas in lists

We use a comma (,) when we write more than two words in a list. We don't usually use a comma before *and*.

I can play the guitar, the piano and the cello.

C Add the missing commas to these sentences.

1 My brother can speak English Turkish and Arabic.
2 Kyle swims runs and rides his bike every week.
3 I go to Spanish classes on Mondays Wednesdays and Fridays.

WRITING

WRITE Imagine that this is your application for the talent show. Complete the missing information. Write a short paragraph. Use commas.

Anyone Can Do It!

Name: ____________

Age: ____________

What can you do?

I can … ____________

____

____

____

____

Write a competition entry

Unit 7 Review

GRAMMAR

A Choose the correct options to complete the sentences.

1 My brother *can* / *can to* swim underwater for three minutes.
2 Lyra can *jump* / *jumps* six meters.
3 A: *Do you can* / *Can you* draw?
B: Yes, I *can* / *draw*.
4 What *do you can* / *can you do*?
5 I *can't drive* / *drive can't* a car, but I *do* / *can* ride a motorcycle.

B Find and correct the mistake in each sentence.

1 Johns brother can play the piano.
2 My sisters names are Jo and Leah.
3 Alexs' hobby is wingsuit flying.
4 What are your parent's names?
5 My friends' an amazing dancer.
6 Paulo's friends' played the cello.

VOCABULARY

A Complete the phrases with the correct letters.

1 p _a_ i _n_ t a p _i_ ct _u_ _r_ _e_
2 p __ __ y the g __ __ t __ r
3 dr __ v __ a c __ __
4 sp __ __ k T __ rk __ sh
5 r __ d __ a b __ c __ c __ e
6 __ l __ y s __ __ c __ r

B Complete the sentences with the adjectives in the box.

boring difficult good long old terrible

1 Niall's a ____________ musician. He can play a lot of instruments.
2 Yoga is ____________. I can't do it.
3 My grandmother is ____________. She's 97.
4 My Spanish is ____________. I can't say anything.
5 I do yoga for a ____________ time every day. I sometimes do it for four hours.
6 I don't like shopping at the grocery store. I think it's ____________.

8 THE HERE AND NOW

Be happy for this moment.
This moment is your life.

Omar Khayyam

A man in front of the Northern Lights, Alaska.

OBJECTIVES

- describe what people are doing
- talk about clothes
- shop for clothes
- write a short message

Work with a partner. Discuss the questions.

1 Look at the picture. Which words from the box describe it?

amazing	boring	beautiful	blue	cold
day	green	warm	night	ugly

2 Would you like to visit this place? Why/Why not?

3 Read the quote. Tell your partner three good things about today.

8.1 What's he doing?

Describe what people are doing

G present progressive **V** verb phrases **P** different ways to pronounce *a*

LISTENING

A PREPARE TO LISTEN Look at the pictures. Match the things (1–6) with the correct picture (a–d).

1 a bench *b*
2 a book ___
3 coffee ___
4 a phone ___
5 a sandwich ___
6 trees ___

B PREPARE TO LISTEN Look at the comic strip again. Choose the correct options.

1 Picture a: The man is talking to a *woman* / *police officer*.
2 Picture b: The man is having lunch *with friends* / *alone*.
3 Picture c: The man is lying *under a tree* / *on a bench*.
4 Picture d: The man is looking at his *watch* / *phone*.

8.1 **C LISTEN FOR THE MAIN IDEA** Listen to a conversation. Put the pictures (a–d) in the correct order.

D SPEAK Work in pairs. Discuss the questions.

1 Do the police have the right man?
2 What item of clothing is the right man wearing?

GRAMMAR

Present progressive

8.2 **A** Listen to a part of the conversation again. Complete the missing words.

Officer A: Can you see the [1] ___?
Officer B: Yes. I'm watching him [2] ___.
Officer A: What's he doing?
Officer B: He's having [3] ___.
Officer A: Is he talking to [4] ___?
Officer B: No, he isn't. He's by himself.
Officer A: Is he in a [5] ___?
Officer B: No, he's sitting on a [6] ___. He's eating a [7] ___ and drinking [8] ___.

B WORK IT OUT Read the conversation in Exercise A. Underline the verbs that end with *-ing*. Choose the correct option to complete the rule.

We use present progressive (verb + *-ing*) to talk about *right now* / *every day*.

C WORK IT OUT Read the examples of the present progressive in the conversation again. Choose the correct options.

Present progressive

1 We make present progressive with *subject* + *be* + *to* + *verb* / *subject* + *be* + *verb* + *-ing*.
2 In questions, the subject (*I, you, he, she, it* …) goes *before* / *after be*.
3 In short answers, we use *subject* + *be* / *subject* + *be* + *verb* + *-ing*.

D WORK IT OUT Complete the table with the correct form of the verbs in the box. Use Exercise A to help you.

eat have sit

Verb (base form)	Spelling rule	Verb + *-ing*
do watch [1] ___	Verb + *-ing*	doing watching [4] ___
live [2] ___	Verb (without *-e*), + *-ing*	living [5] ___
get [3] ___	Verb (add extra last consonant) + *-ing*	getting [6] ___

E Go to the **Grammar Hub** on **page VIII**.

F SPEAK Work in pairs. Choose a picture from the comic strip but don't tell your partner which one. Describe it to your partner. Which picture is it?

A: I can see a man.
B: What's he doing?
A: He's sitting on a bench. He's …
B: Is it picture …?

VOCABULARY

Verb phrases

A Choose the correct verbs to complete the phrases. Use each verb only once.

go have look meet read take talk watch

1 ______________ a friend

2 ______________ at your phone

3 ______________ a selfie

4 ______________ a good time

5 ______________ the newspaper

6 ______________ a movie

7 ______________ to the bank

8 ______________ to a friend

B Match the verbs from Exercise A with the words and phrases.

1 ____have____ lunch / a meeting / coffee
2 ______________ TV / a soccer game / someone do something
3 ______________ a book / a message / a magazine
4 ______________ out / to the library / shopping
5 ______________ to a teacher / on the phone / about something
6 ______________ a photo / a break / a taxi
7 ______________ at a picture / in the mirror / at someone
8 ______________ someone at a party / at nine o'clock / at the station

PRONUNCIATION

Different ways to pronounce *a*

8.3 **A** Listen and repeat the words in the table.

/æ/	/eɪ/	/ɔː/	/ɑ /
have	take	walk	watch
________	________	________	________
________	________	________	________

8.4 **B** Listen to the words in the box and put them in the correct place in the table.

call catch fall match play stay want wash

8.5 **C** Listen and complete the questions.

1 What do you ______________: ball games or board games?
2 Who do you ______________ to every day?
3 What do you usually ______________ for lunch?
4 What do you ______________ to ______________: a soccer game or a movie?

D **SPEAK** Work with a partner. Ask the questions in Exercise C. Give full answers.

SPEAKING

Work in pairs. Student A – Look at the instructions below. Student B – Go to the **Communication Hub** on **page XXII**.

Student A

- Look at the picture.
- Describe the people and what they are doing to your partner.
- Listen to your partner's description of their picture.
- Find six differences.

Describe what people are doing

8.2 The gray coat

Talk about clothes

V clothes **P** vowel sounds: /iː/, /ɜː/, /uː/ and /ɔː/ **S** identifying key words **G** adjective order

VOCABULARY

Clothes

A Look at Person 1 in the picture. What clothes is he wearing? Choose words from the box to complete the description.

shorts sneakers socks T-shirt

He's wearing a white [1] ______ and blue [2] ______. He's wearing red [3] ______ and white [4] ______. He also has a green backpack.

B Go to the **Vocabulary Hub** on **page XVIII**.

C **SPEAK** Work in pairs. Choose someone in the picture. Ask and answer questions. Who is your partner describing?

A: She's wearing a dress.
B: Is she wearing a hat?
A: Yes, she is.

PRONUNCIATION

Vowel sounds: /iː/, /ɜː/, /uː/ and /ɔː/

8.6 **A** Complete the sentences with a word in the box that has the same sound as the underlined letters. Listen and check.

a coat ~~a hat~~ jeans a shirt shorts a suit

1 Hannah's wearing a cap. Izzie's wearing *a hat*.
2 Ally's wearing a skirt and ______.
3 Paulo's wearing ______ and shoes.

8.7 **B** Listen to the words for clothes. Then listen and repeat.

jeans shirt shoes shorts

8.8 **C** Match the words in the box with the correct vowel sound in questions 1–4. Then listen and check.

bird clean do door green sports who word

1 /iː/ jeans ______ ______
2 /ɜː/ shirt ______ ______
3 /uː/shoes ______ ______
4 /ɔː/ shorts ______ ______

D **SPEAK** Work in pairs. Look around you. Describe different people.

A: Eva's wearing jeans. *B: Elliot's wearing a shirt.*

READING

A **PREPARE TO READ** Look at the picture at the top of the page again. What are the people doing?

B **READ FOR KEY WORDS** Read the messages and look at the picture. Which person (1–11) is Claus? Which person is Imogen?

Claus ___ Imogen ___

Identifying key words

Looking for key words can help you understand the topic of a text or sentence quickly.

I'm wearing a gray ***sweatshirt****. [Topic = clothes]*

Claus

Hi Claus, I'm at the station. Where are you?

I'm here, too. I have the bag, but I can't see you. What are you wearing?

An old blue sweatshirt and a yellow cap.

Sorry, I can't see you. Where are you?

I'm standing near the store. What are you wearing?

A long gray coat.

I think I can see you. Are you wearing a red cap?

Yes, I am.

I can see you! I think the police are watching.

The police? Why are the police watching?

Something's happening at the bank. It's on the radio. The police are looking for a man with a gray coat and a bag with a lot of money.

I have a bag, but it doesn't have any money in it! It's your bag ... from the restaurant last night.

I know, thank you! I'm coming over to you now.

C READ FOR SPECIFIC INFORMATION Read the messages again. Answer the questions.

1 Can Imogen see Claus when she arrives at the station?
2 Can Claus see Imogen?
3 Where is Imogen?
4 Why are the police watching Claus?
5 Is Claus the man the police are looking for?
6 Is the bag Claus's bag or Imogen's bag?

D READ FOR DETAIL Read the messages again. Find and correct the five mistakes in the summary.

Claus is at the park. He's meeting Imogen. Claus has a blue coat and a bag. The police are looking for a man with a gray sweatshirt and a bag. Claus has Imogen's coat. There is a lot of money in the bag.

GRAMMAR

Adjective order

A Read the messages in Reading Exercise B again. Underline the adjectives of size or age. Circle the adjectives of color.

B WORK IT OUT Read these sentences from the messages. Choose the correct option to complete the rules.

Adjective order

I'm wearing an old blue sweatshirt and a yellow cap.
I'm wearing a long gray coat.

1 We *can* / *can't* put more than one adjective before a noun.
2 The color adjective usually goes *before* / *after* the adjective for size or age.

C Go to the **Grammar Hub** on **page VIII**.

D PRACTICE Rewrite the sentences and add the extra adjectives in parentheses.

1 It's a blue shirt. (new)
It's a new blue shirt.
2 She's wearing an old dress. (green)
______
3 I have a new hat. (red)
______
4 That's a blue skirt. (long)
______

E SPEAK Work in pairs. Describe the clothes in the pictures.

a

b

c

d

big long short small

She's wearing a long yellow coat.

SPEAKING HUB

A PREPARE Imagine you are in these situations. What are you wearing? What are you doing? Write notes.

a You're in the park in the summer.

b You're traveling for business.

c You're at a concert.

B PRACTICE Work in pairs. Choose one of the situations in Exercise A. Your partner is trying to find you, but they can't. Have a phone conversation and describe what you are wearing and what you are doing.

A: What are you wearing?
B: I'm wearing a long red skirt, a white hat and sunglasses.

C REPEAT Find a new partner. Choose a new situation and describe what you're wearing and what you're doing.

Talk about clothes

Café Hub

8.3 Too loud

F – shop for clothes

COMPREHENSION

A Watch the video and answer the questions.

1 Where are Gaby and Lucy?
2 Who buys something? Why?

B Are the sentences true (T) or false (F)? Correct the false sentences.

1 Gaby is waiting for Lucy. T / F
2 Lucy says Gaby's hair is bad. T / F
3 The cap seller likes the music. T / F
4 Gaby wants to buy a cap. T / F
5 There's a blue cap. T / F
6 The caps are one size. T / F
7 Caps cost £10. T / F
8 Gaby needs a small cap. T / F

C Watch the video again and check your answers to Exercise B.

D What do you think of the music? Choose an adjective from the box or use your own ideas.

amazing bad good horrible OK

USEFUL PHRASES

A Match the phrases (1–4) with the pictures (a–d).

1 It's not bad. It's just different. ___
2 Oh, look over there. ___
3 She's joking! ___
4 I have a surprise for you. ___

B Which useful phrase means *She's not serious*?

C Watch the video again and check your answers to Exercises A and B.

a

b

c

d

GABY SAM LUCY

FUNCTIONAL LANGUAGE

Shopping for clothes

A Read the conversation and underline the correct options.

Sales person	Lucy
Can I [1]*see / help*?	We're [2]*just / only* looking, thanks.
No problem.	Actually, I'm [3]*looking / waiting* for a cap.
Sure. We have caps. Lots of them!	Great! Do you have a blue [4]*type / one*?
Yes, we have blue. What [5]*size / color* would you like: small, medium or [6]*big / large*?	Can I [7]*want / have* a medium, please?
Of course.	Perfect. How [8]*much / money* is it?
Ten pounds.	

B ▶ 00:45–01:59 Watch part of the video and check your answers.

PRONUNCIATION

8.9 **A** Listen to the conversation and notice how the underlined words are stressed.

Sales person:	Can I help you?
Customer:	I'm just looking, thanks.
Sales person:	OK, no problem.
Customer:	Actually, I'm looking for a T-shirt. Do you have a red one?
Sales person:	Yes. What size would you like? Small, medium or large?
Customer:	Can I have a large, please?
Sales person:	Of course.
Customer:	How much is it?
Sales person:	Seventeen dollars.

8.9 **B** Listen again and repeat the conversation. Copy the stress.

C SPEAK Work in pairs. Practice the conversation.

SPEAKING

A PLAN You are a sales person. Look at the clothes and decide how much each item costs.

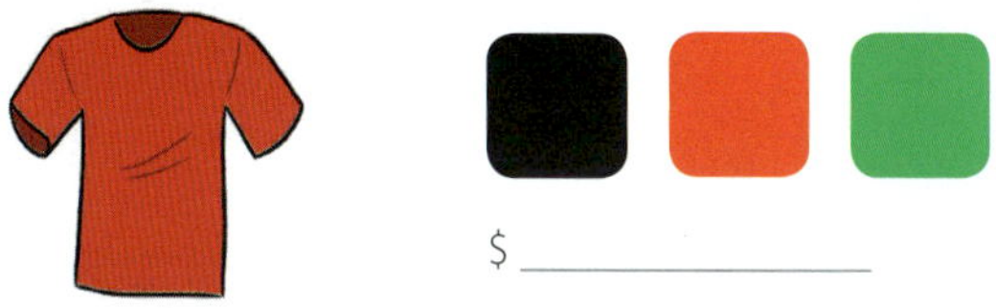

$ ________

$ ________

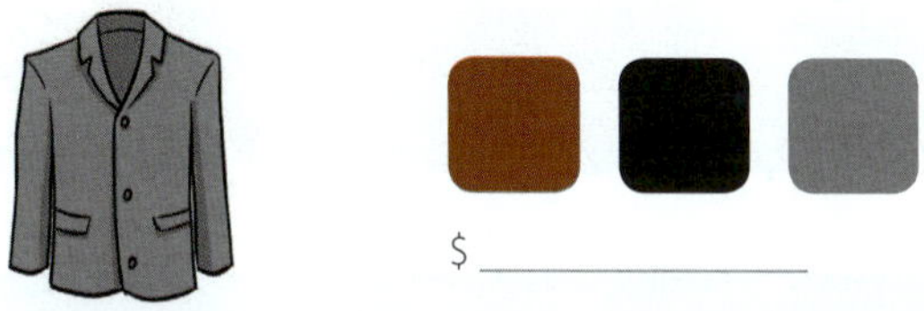

$ ________

$ ________

$ ________

$ ________

B PREPARE You are shopping for clothes. Decide what you want to buy, the color and the size you need.

C PRACTICE Work in pairs. Decide who is the sales person and who is the customer. Have a conversation and buy the clothes you want. Use the conversation in Pronunciation Exercise A to help you.

D REPEAT Change roles and have a new conversation.

Shop for clothes

8 Writing

Write a short message

W – using *also* and *too*

A Read the text message conversation between two friends. Choose the correct image for where Mia is.

Hi Mia. What are you doing?

Hi Petra. I'm at a barbecue at Amy's house. It's so nice and sunny today!

Oh great! Who are you with?

I'm with Greg. Lilly's here, too. They're making the food.

What are you doing?!

I'm sitting in the sun and talking to Amy. Do you want to come over?

I can't. I'm shopping with my sister right now. Also, I have to work later. Maybe next time 😉.

a

b

B Read the messages again. Answer the questions.

1. Where's Mia?
2. Who's with Mia?
3. What are Greg and Lilly doing?
4. What's Mia doing?
5. Why can't Petra go?

Using *also* and *too*

We use *also* and *too* to say that something is true about more than one person or thing. We usually put *also* at the beginning of a sentence or before the verb. We always put *too* at the end of a sentence.

Also, I have to work later.

Lilly's here, too.

WRITING

WRITE Write a text message conversation between two friends. Choose a situation from the pictures in Exercise A or use your own ideas.

Write a short message

Unit 8 Review

GRAMMAR

A Complete the conversation using short answers and the verbs in parentheses in the present progressive.

A: What [1] ___are___ you ___doing___ (*do*)?
B: I [2] __________ __________ (*eat*) lunch.
A: [3] __________ Michael __________ (*have*) lunch with you?
B: No, he [4] __________. He [5] __________ __________ (*work*) in the library.
A: Who [6] __________ he __________ (*work*) with?
B: He [7] __________ __________ (*not work*) with anyone.

B Order the words to make sentences.

1. is / this / blue / new / my / sweatshirt
   This is my new blue sweatshirt.
2. has / an / gray / hat / he / old
   __________.
3. wearing / a / long / dress / white / she's
   __________.
4. a / short / coat / brown / the man / wearing / is
   __________.

VOCABULARY

A Join the halves to make sentences.

1. I'm going
2. We're watching
3. Aki and Darren are meeting
4. Luke's reading
5. My sister is having
6. Geri is talking
7. Yannick is looking
8. Luke's taking

a. to her friend on the phone.
b. a photo with his new camera.
c. to a café.
d. at the bus station.
e. TV at home.
f. at clothes in a store.
g. lunch.
h. a magazine.

B Complete the words for clothes.

1. d __ e __ __
2. sw __ __ __ s __ __ __ __
3. h __ __
4. j __ a __ s
5. s __ __ e __
6. sn __ a __ e __ __

9 LOOKING BACK

A statue at Mount Nemrut, Turkey.

OBJECTIVES

- talk about famous people from the past
- talk about people's achievements
- make recommendations
- write a short biography

Work with a partner. Discuss the questions.

1 Look at the picture. Do you want to visit this place?

2 Who is your favorite person from history? Why do you like them?

3 Where can you see statues of famous people in your country?

9.1 Famous faces

Talk about famous people from the past

G simple past: *was/were* **V** dates and years **P** *was he / was she*

LISTENING

A PREPARE TO LISTEN Look at the pictures in *A visit to Madame Tussauds*. Do you know these famous people? Why are they famous?

9.1 **B LISTEN FOR SPECIFIC INFORMATION** Listen and write the missing years (a–d) in *A visit to Madame Tussauds*.

9.1 **C LISTEN FOR SPECIFIC INFORMATION** Listen again and complete the information below.

1 AUDREY HEPBURN
Country: 1 ____________
Jobs: 2 ____________
3 ____________
4 ____________
She was famous for her 5 ____________ clothes.

2 WILLIAM SHAKESPEARE
Country: 6 ____________
Jobs: 7 ____________
8 ____________
9 ____________ of words in everyday English come from his work.

3 MARIE TUSSAUD
Country: 10 ____________
Job: Famous for 11 ____________ in London. 12 ____________

4 NELSON MANDELA
Country: 13 ____________
Job: President for 14 ____________ years.

A VISIT TO MADAME TUSSAUDS

In cities all over the world – in London, Paris, New York and New Delhi – people come to Madame Tussauds to see waxwork statues of famous people from the past and present. Why were they famous? Were they actors? Writers? Or inspirational leaders? Enjoy a visit to Madame Tussauds to find out more about these famous faces.

MAY 4TH
a ____________

APRIL 26TH
b ____________

DECEMBER 1ST
c ____________

JULY 18TH
d ____________

GRAMMAR

Simple past: *was/were*

A Read the examples from *A visit to Madame Tussauds*. Underline examples of *was* and *were*.

1 Why were they famous?
2 Were they actors?
3 Was she a model?
4 Her movies were very popular.
5 Why was he famous?
6 He was a famous writer.
7 He wasn't just a writer.
8 Photographs weren't common.

B **WORK IT OUT** Complete the table with the sentences from Exercise A.

was/were	Singular	Plural
positive	______	______
negative	______	______
yes/no questions	______	______
wh- questions	______	______

C **WORK IT OUT** Look at Exercises A and B. Complete the rules with *was, wasn't, were* or *weren't*.

Simple past: *was/were*

1 ______ is the past form of *is*. ______ is the past form of *are*.
2 ______ is the past form of *isn't*. ______ is the past form of *aren't*.
3 We make *yes/no* questions with ______ or ______ + subject.
4 We make *wh-* questions with a question word + ______ or ______.

D Go to the **Grammar Hub** on **page X**.

E **SPEAK** Work in pairs. Who was your favorite celebrity when you were young? Why were they famous?

VOCABULARY

Dates and years

9.2 **A** Match the numbers (1–6) with the words in the box. Listen and check.

fifth first fourth second sixth third

1 1st ______
2 2nd ______
3 3rd ______
4 4th ______
5 5th ______
6 6th ______

9.3 **B** Listen and write the numbers that you hear.

a ___ b ___ c ___ d ___ e ___
f ___ g ___ h ___ i ___ j ___

9.4 **C** Listen and circle the years you hear.

a 1948 / 1958
b 1909 / 1999
c 2014 / 2040
d 1564 / 1546
e 2002 / 2012
f 1800 / 1900

D **SPEAK** Stand up and walk around. Say the day and month of your birthday to each other. Then stand in order according to your birthday.

PRONUNCIATION

was he / was she

9.5 **A** Read and listen. Draw a line (‿) to show the linked words.

1 Was he a writer?
2 Was she a writer?
3 Where was he born?
4 Where was she born?

9.6 **B** Listen to each question and choose the words you hear.

1 *Was he* / *Was she* an artist?
2 *Was he* / *Was she* an actor?
3 Why *was he* / *was she* famous?
4 When *was he* / *was she* born?

SPEAKING

A **PREPARE** Think of a famous person from the past. Complete the information about him or her.

Man or woman? ______

Country? ______

Job? ______

When were they famous? ______

Why were they famous? ______

B **DISCUSS** Work in pairs. Describe your famous person. Don't say the name of the person. Ask your partner questions. Who is it?

A: He was a singer in The Beatles.
B: John Lennon?

C **REPORT** Tell the class about your famous person.

Talk about famous people from the past

V everyday verbs S scanning G simple past: regular verbs P past tense endings: /d/, /t/ and /ɪd/

VOCABULARY
Everyday verbs

A Look at the pictures. Match the phrases in the box with the correct pictures.

collect stamps design a building help a friend paint a picture receive a present start to run study in college travel to the city

1 ______________

2 ______________

3 ______________

4 ______________

5 ______________

6 ______________

7 ______________

8 ______________

B **SPEAK** Work in pairs. Use the verbs to make sentences that are true for you.

A: I collect CDs.

B: I travel to Rome every fall for work.

READING

A **PREPARE TO READ** Which heroes from children's stories can you name?

B **READ FOR GIST** Read *Goodnight stories for rebel girls*. Choose the correct options to complete the summary.

Goodnight stories for rebel girls is about ***real women / women in children's stories***.

Scanning

When you scan a text, you read it to look for specific information. Scanning helps you find information more quickly. Look for key words, names, dates and percentages.

GOODNIGHT STORIES for REBEL GIRLS

What were your favorite stories when you were young? Who were your heroes? How many were girls?

In 2011, the University of Florida studied the number of male and female characters in children's storybooks. There were male characters in every book. But 25 percent had no female characters. And in 37 percent of the books, the female characters didn't talk.

Two Italian women, Elena Favilli and Francesca Cavallo, decided to change this. They wanted to make a book of stories about real women. They asked people for money online to make the book. They received over a million dollars! Here are some of the women in their book:

Maria Sibylla Merian (1647–1717)
Merian was a scientist. She was born in Frankfurt in Germany. When she was a child, she collected butterflies and insects. She discovered many new things about them. She traveled to South America and painted beautiful pictures of nature.

Ada Lovelace (1815–1852)
Lovelace was an English mathematician. She didn't study at public school or college. She studied at home with a teacher. When she was 12, she designed a flying machine. Also, she was the first computer programmer in the world.

Wangari Maathai (1940–2011)
Maathai was a Kenyan politician. She studied at universities in the US and in Germany. She wanted to help people in Kenya, so she and a group of women started to plant trees. They planted hundreds of trees and the trees helped people and nature. She received the Nobel Peace Prize in 2004.

C READ FOR DETAIL Are these statements true (T) or false (F)?

1 There are female characters in all children's books. *T / F*
2 Some female characters in children's books don't say anything. *T / F*
3 The writers of *Goodnight stories for rebel girls* are men. *T / F*
4 Maria Sibylla Merian was a mathematician. *T / F*
5 Ada Lovelace was a computer programmer. *T / F*
6 Wangari Maathai was the winner of an important prize. *T / F*

D SPEAK Work in groups. Discuss the questions.

1 Do you think that this book was a good idea? Why/Why not?
2 Do you think that this book is good for boys, too? Why/Why not?
3 Do girls and boys read the same or different books? Why/Why not?

GRAMMAR

Simple past: regular verbs

A Read the introduction to the article again. Write the simple past: form of the verbs.

1 study ____________ 4 ask ____________
2 decide ____________ 5 receive ____________
3 want ____________

B Read the section about Ada Lovelace again and underline the negative verb.

C WORK IT OUT Match the two parts of each rule (1–4) with (a–d). Use the examples in Exercises A and B to help you.

Simple past: regular verbs	
1 We add *-ed*	a we use *did* + *not* (*didn't*) before the verb.
2 We add *-d*	b to verbs ending in *-e*.
3 With verbs ending in *-y*,	c we cut the *-y* and add *-ied*.
4 To form the negative,	d to most verbs.

D Go to the Grammar Hub on page X.

PRONUNCIATION

Past tense endings: /d/, /t/ and /ɪd/

9.7 **A** Read and listen to the verbs. Notice how we say the endings.

/d/	/t/	/ɪd/
studied	helped	wanted

9.8 **B** Listen to the verbs and add them to the table in Exercise A.

1 decided
2 asked
3 designed
4 lived
5 started
6 talked
7 collected
8 traveled

SPEAKING HUB

Work in groups. Group A – Stay on this page. Group B – Go to the Communication Hub on page XXII.

A PREPARE Complete the sentences with the past tense of verbs from the box. Then choose the correct information (a, b or c) to complete the sentences.

discover live receive start

1 Larry Page and Segey Brin ____________ the company Google in …
a 1998. b 2001. c 2008.
2 John Couch Adams ____________ the planet Neptune in …
a 1696. b 1846. c 1906.
3 William Shakespeare ____________ in England in the … century.
a 15th b 16th c 17th
4 Malala Yousafzai ____________ the Nobel Peace Prize in …
a 2001. b 2014. c 2016.

B PRACTICE Read your sentences to Group B. They will check your answers.

C PRACTICE Listen to Group B's sentences. Check their answers.

Correct sentences:

1 Ibn Battuta **traveled** from Morocco to China in the **14th century**.
2 Gabriel García Márquez **received** the Nobel Prize in Literature in **1982**.
3 Neil Armstrong **walked** on the moon in **1969**.
4 Steve Jobs and Steve Wozniak **designed** the first personal computers in **1976**.

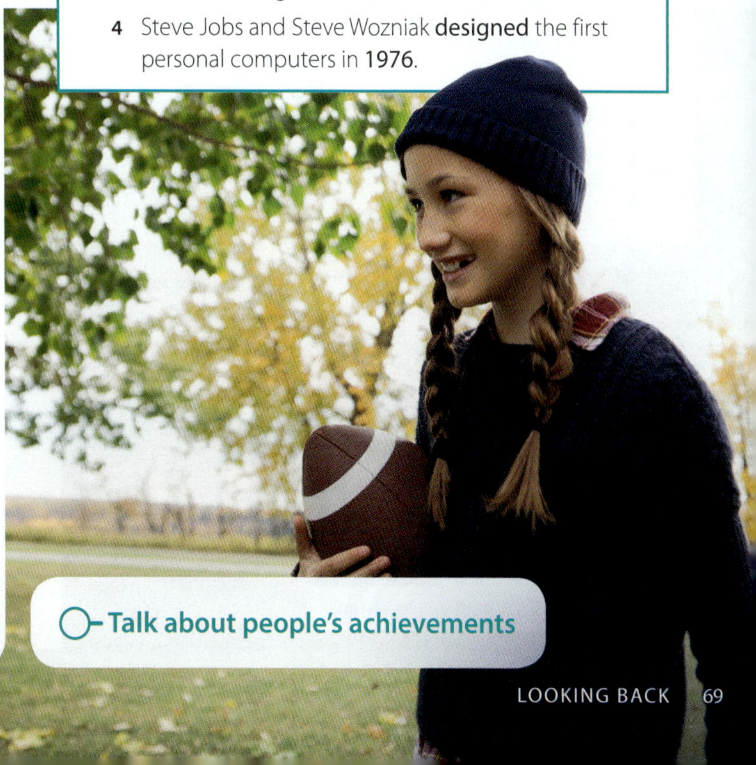

Talk about people's achievements

Café Hub

9.3 Pizza Roma

F– make recommendations

COMPREHENSION

A ▶ **00.10–01:14** Watch the first part of the video and choose the correct options to complete the sentences.

1 Sam is *opening* / *closing* the café.
2 Sam *knows* / *doesn't know* Metal Train.
3 Gaby *loves* / *hates* pizza.
4 Pizza Roma is *terrible* / *amazing*.
5 Pizza Roma has *big* / *small* pizzas.
6 The pizzas are *expensive* / *cheap*.
7 Pizza Roma is *near* / *far from* Sam's Café.

B ▶ **01:15–01:34** Watch part of the video and choose the correct set of directions from Sam's Café to Pizza Roma.

1  ☐

2 

☐

3  ☐

C ▶ **01:35–03:00** Watch the second part of the video. Discuss the questions.

1 What was Gaby's pizza like?
2 Did she eat it?
3 Where did she buy it?
4 What does Gaby eat?
5 What does Lucy do?
6 Where was Lucy's pizza from?

USEFUL PHRASES

A Who says it? Gaby (G) or Sam (S)?

1 I'm afraid I'm closing now. ______
2 Hey! That's a nice cap! ______
3 Ah, I see. ______
4 It's not far. ______
5 It's next to the station. ______
6 I've got it, thanks! ______

Glossary

shop (n) (British) = store (n) (American)

B Match the useful phrases in Exercise A with the meanings.

I understand. [1]______ [2]______
I'm sorry … [3]______
It's near here. [4]______
I like your … [5]______

C Replace the underlined phrases with useful phrases from Exercise A.

Gaby: Hi, Sam. [1]<u>I like your</u> T-shirt.
Sam: Thanks. It's from my friend's shop.
Gaby: Where's her shop?
Sam: Oh, [2]<u>it's near here</u>. Just go out the café, turn left, turn left again and it's on your right.
Gaby: Left, left, right. [3]<u>I understand</u>, thanks!
Sam: [4]<u>I'm sorry.</u> I'm going to my yoga class now. It starts in five minutes.
Gaby: Ah, [5]<u>I understand</u>! Bye!

FUNCTIONAL LANGUAGE

Making recommendations

A ▶ Complete the phrases with the words in the box. Then watch the video again and check your answers.

Don't   Do you know   There's   You should

Asking for a recommendation

[1]______ / **Is there** a good restaurant near here?

Giving a recommendation

[2]______ / **I know** a really good pizza restaurant. It's called Pizza Roma.

I was there last week. And the pizza was amazing. It was really big and really cheap.

[3]______ / **Why don't you** try it.

[4]______ / **I wouldn't** go to Pizza Nova! I went there last week. The pizza was bad! It was really small and really expensive.

B Circle the correct options to complete the conversation.

Liz: [1]*Do you know* / *There's* a good café near here?
Mark: Do you like big breakfasts?
Liz: I love big breakfasts.
Mark: OK, [2]*why don't you* / *there's* a really good café. It's called Tom's Café. I was there this morning. The breakfast is [3]*amazing* / *horrible*. It's really big and really cheap. [4]You *should* / *shouldn't* go there.
Liz: Thanks! Don't go to Rachel's Café. I went there yesterday. The coffee was [5]*amazing* / *terrible*. It was really small and really bad.
Mark: Oh, I see. Thanks.

GABY

SAM

LUCY

PRONUNCIATION

9.9 **A** Listen to the conversation and notice how the underlined words are stressed.

Frank: Do you know a good restaurant near here?
Emily: Do you like sushi?
Frank: I love Japanese food.
Emily: There's a really good Japanese restaurant. It's called Sushirama.
Frank: Great.
Emily: I was there last week. And the sushi was amazing. It was really fresh. You should try it. Don't go to Suzy's Sushi! It's really bad.

9.9 **B** Listen again and repeat the conversation. Copy the stress.

SPEAKING

A PLAN Work in pairs. Read *Restaurants near you*. Discuss the questions.

1 Which restaurant(s) would you like to go to? Why?
2 Which restaurant(s) would you **not** like to go to? Why?

B PREPARE Rewrite the conversation in Pronunciation Exercise A.

- Replace the blue phrases with new ideas from the Functional language section.
- Replace the words in red using the ideas in the reviews below.
- Create some directions and include three or more useful phrases.

C PRACTICE Work in pairs. Practice and then perform your conversation in front of the class.

D REPEAT Choose different restaurants. Change roles and have a new conversation.

Restaurants near you

Moo Burger Bar
★★★★☆
Great fries!

Bob's Burgers
★☆☆☆☆
Terrible burgers, bad fries.

Puk Yuk Thai
★★★★★
Amazing! Best Thai food in town.

Bangkok House
★☆☆☆☆
Expensive Thai food.

Pierre's French cuisine
★☆☆☆☆
Bad service. Terrible food.

Paris mon amour
★★★★★
Amazing French food.

Make recommendations

9 Writing — Write a short biography

W – organizing your notes

A Work in pairs. What can you see in the pictures? What is the connection between them?

B Read the description and complete the notes.

Leonardo da Vinci

Leonardo da Vinci was born near Florence in Italy in 1452. He was an artist, a mathematician, a scientist, a musician and a writer. He is famous for his paintings, but he also designed machines. He painted the famous *Mona Lisa*. He painted this picture in 1503 and it is now in the Louvre Museum in Paris, France. It is a picture of a woman with a beautiful smile.

Name:	*Occupation(s):*
Birth date:	*Why famous?*
Birth place:	*Famous painting:*

Organizing your notes

When you are planning your writing, think about how to organize your notes. In a biography, you can start with personal information (date and place of birth), describe their job, say why they are famous and finally describe one thing they are famous for.

C Read the notes below. Number the information in the best order for a description.

- ☐ artist
- ☐ changed the world of art
- 1 Pablo Picasso
- ☐ Cubism, new style of painting
- ☐ Málaga, Spain
- ☐ 1881

WRITING

A PLAN Add any more details that you know about Picasso. Decide where to write this information.

B WRITE Write a description using the information in Exercise C. Compare with a partner.

Write a short biography

Unit 9 Review

GRAMMAR

A Complete the sentences with the correct past form of *be*.

1 Shakespeare ________ a writer and a poet.
2 Pablo Picasso and Marie Tussaud ________ artists.
3 A: ________ Maya Angelou a poet?
B: Yes, she ________.
4 A: ________ Gandhi a scientist?
B: No, he ________.
5 There ________ any phone selfies in the 1700s.
6 There ________ a black president of South Africa before Nelson Mandela.

B Complete the sentences with past tense forms in the positive (+) or negative (-).

1 Last weekend, I ________ (+ *stay*) at home and I ________ (+ *paint*) my bedroom.
2 Tamara ________ (– *pick up*) her computer from the store, but she ________ (+ *organize*) her files.
3 Omar ________ (– *visit*) his grandma, but he ________ (+ *call*) her at home.

VOCABULARY

A Complete the sentences with words for ordinal numbers.

1 We live in the *twenty-first* (*21st*) century.
2 Shakespeare lived in the ________ (*16th*) century.
3 March is the ________ (*3rd*) month of the year.
4 George Washington was the ________ (*1st*) US president.

B Complete the description with the past form of a verb from the box.

be	help	return	start	study	travel

Marco Polo

Marco Polo was born in Venice in 1254. He and his father [1] ________ to China. They [2] ________ their journey in 1271 when Marco Polo [3] ________ 17 years old. The journey was long and difficult. Marco Polo stayed in China for many years and [4] ________ Chinese language and culture. When Marco [5] ________ to Italy 26 years later, his friend [6] ________ him to write a book about his experiences.

10 IT'S HISTORY

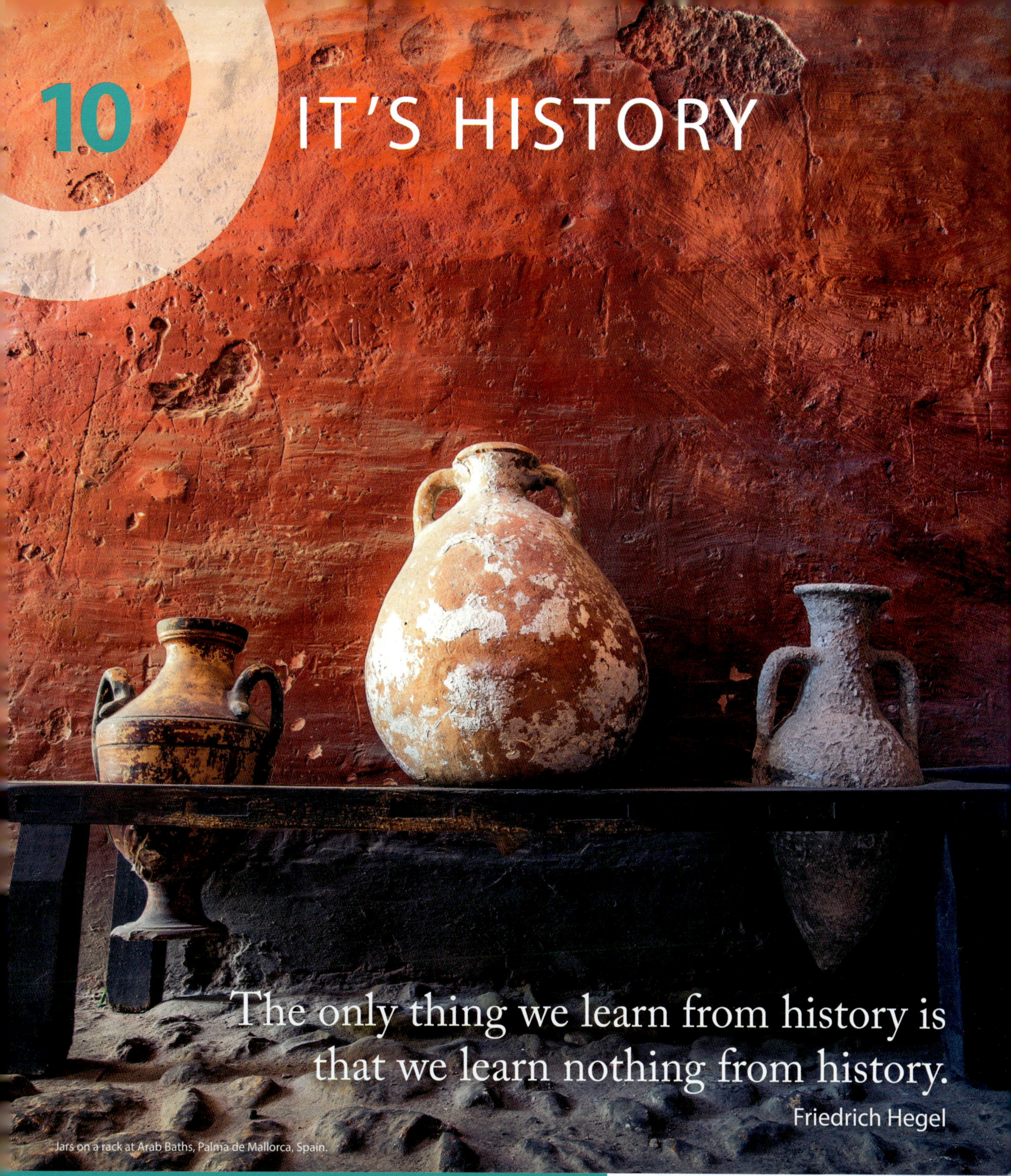

> The only thing we learn from history is that we learn nothing from history.
>
> Friedrich Hegel

Jars on a rack at Arab Baths, Palma de Mallorca, Spain.

OBJECTIVES

- talk about past events
- talk about past experiences
- talk about what you did on the weekend
- write a paragraph about a past event

Work with a partner. Discuss the questions.

1 Look at the picture. What can you see?

2 Choose words to describe the objects in the picture.

beautiful boring important interesting old new useful

3 Are you interested in history?

10.1 Precious finds

Talk about past events

G simple past: irregular verbs V time phrases P vowel sounds: /ɔː/ and /oʊ/

A HISTORY OF THE WORLD IN 100 OBJECTS

The British Museum in London has a lot of important objects from the past. A few years ago, the museum director started an interesting project. He **chose** 100 objects from the museum to tell a history of the world. Here are just four of the objects. What do they tell us about the past?

HAND AXE

1.2–1.4 million years old, Olduvai Gorge, Tanzania

Scientists **found** many of these hand axes in different regions of Africa. The first humans didn't have metal. They **made** these axes from stone and used them to cut meat and wood.

TWO-HEADED SNAKE

15th–16th century, Aztec Empire, Mexico

600 years ago, the Aztec people **gave** this bright blue snake to the Aztec Emperor. It **took** a lot of time and skill to make this beautiful object. We think the Emperor **wore** it to show how important he was.

GOLD MODEL CHARIOT

5th–4th century BCE, Tajikistan

The Persians **built** many new roads across their country. The man in this model **went** from town to town in his chariot. He collected money for the king and carried important messages for people.

BANKNOTE

CE 135, China

In the 2nd century, Chinese people **bought** and **sold** things using these banknotes. They made banknotes from paper. Before this, people used coins. This banknote was the same as 1,000 coins. The Emperor's name was on these notes to show that they were real.

READING

A PREDICT Look at the pictures above. Which object do you think is most interesting?

B READ FOR GIST Read the introduction to *A history of the world in 100 objects*. Choose the best option to complete the summary.

The museum director chose these objects because …

1 they show us what life was like in the past.
2 they tell us about important events.
3 they belonged to important people.

C READ FOR MAIN IDEA Read the text and match each sentence with an object from the text.

1 This was the first kind of paper money. ______________
2 People used this to cut things. ______________
3 They made it for an important person. ______________
4 This was a way to travel around the country. ______________

D SPEAK Work in pairs. Ask and answer questions about each object.

1 Where is it from? 2 How old is it? 3 What is it for?

E SPEAK Work in pairs. Discuss the questions.

1 Which objects are beautiful? Which are useful?
2 Which objects do you use today?

GRAMMAR

Simple past: irregular verbs

A Read *A history of the world in 100 objects* again. Complete the table with words in bold in the article.

Irregular verb	Past form	Irregular verb	Past form
build	1 ______	go	6 ______
buy	2 ______	make	7 ______
choose	3 ______	sell	8 ______
find	4 ______	take	9 ______
give	5 ______	wear	10 ______

B Read the text again. There is one example of the simple past negative. Find and underline it.

C WORK IT OUT Choose the correct options to complete the rules. Use *A history of the world in 100 objects* to help you.

Simple past: irregular verbs

1 Irregular verbs *have* / *don't have* -*ed* in the past.
2 We *add* / *don't add* -*s* to the third person singular in the past.
3 We use *didn't* + verb / verb + -*ed* + *not* in negative sentences.

A lot of common verbs have irregular past tense endings. See the irregular verbs list on page IV.

D Go to the Grammar Hub on page XII.

VOCABULARY
Time phrases

A Read the short text below. Underline time phrases with *in*, *last* and *ago*.

We studied this painting in our art class last year. The artist, Zhang Zeduan, painted this picture 1,000 years ago. It shows everyday life in China in the 12th century.

B Write the time expressions in the table.

the 12th century ~~fifty years~~ 1600 a long time month an hour Friday the past week

Ago	Last	In
fifty years		

C Complete the sentences with *in*, *last* or *ago*.

1 A hundred years ______________ people didn't have cell phones.

2 Women wore long dresses ______________ the 15th century.

3 People found some old gold coins here ______________ year.

D SPEAK Work in pairs. Describe how life was different in the past. Use the topics in the box to help you.

clothes homes money shopping transportation

A: How was life different in the past?
B: People didn't buy clothes in a store very frequently. They made clothes at home.

PRONUNCIATION
Vowel sounds: /ɔː/ and /oʊ/

A 10.1 Read and listen to the vowel sound in these words. Listen again and repeat.

/ɔː/	bought	saw	tall	walk
/oʊ/	chose	go	nose	phone

B 10.2 Circle words with the same sound as *bought*. Underline words with the same sound as *chose*. Then listen and check.

floor four know slow show talk toe wore

C SPEAK Work in pairs. Describe five things you did last week. Use the past tense form of the verbs in the box.

buy call choose see talk tell walk

A: I walked to school.
B: I bought some new shoes.

SPEAKING

A PREPARE Work in groups. Choose five objects that explain what life is like in the 21st century and why they are important.

smartphone *talk with friends*

1 ______________ ______________

2 ______________ ______________

3 ______________ ______________

4 ______________ ______________

5 ______________ ______________

B PRESENT Imagine you are in the 25th century. Explain what life was like in the 21st century. Use your ideas from Exercise A.

C DISCUSS Work with another group. Can you agree on the five most important objects?

Talk about past events

10.2 Family treasures

Talk about past experiences

V life events **S** identifying reasons **G** simple past questions **P** final consonant /t/ and /d/

VOCABULARY

Life events

A Read the descriptions. Underline the verbs in the simple past.

This is a picture of me and my girlfriend, Susan. I met her on the first day of college. This is the day we finished college.

I wrote a short story for the school competition when I was in school and I won first prize!

This is a picture of me and my husband on the day we got married! It was in the Bahamas – it was really beautiful.

This is the day I passed my driving test! I was really happy. This sports car belonged to my uncle and I drove it home after the test.

B Match the two parts of each phrase (1–8) with (a–h) to make collocations from Exercise A. Use each verb (1–8) only once.

1	pass	a	a person
2	meet	b	a story
3	finish	c	a car
4	write	d	a prize
5	belong	e	to someone
6	get	f	a test
7	win	g	college
8	drive	h	married

C SPEAK Describe three important events in your life. Say when they happened.

A: I passed my driving test three years ago.
B: I finished college in 2010.

LISTENING

A PREDICT Look at the pictures. What do you think is the same about all the objects?

10.3 **B LISTEN FOR GIST** Listen to three people speaking about the objects. Write the name of the person (Janine, Alfie or Isabel) under the object they talk about.

Identifying reasons

The phrases *that's the reason* or *that's why* come **after** the reason. The reason is in the sentence **before**.

She gave me the camera *That's why* I became a photographer.

10.3 **C LISTEN FOR DETAIL** Listen again and complete the table with information from the podcast.

	Object	Who gave it to the speaker?	When did they give it?	Why is it important?
1	*silver pocket watch*			
2				
3				

D SPEAK Tell your partner about an object that is important to you. Did someone give it to you? Did you get it for a special reason?

My parents gave me a necklace on my 18th birthday.

GRAMMAR
Simple past questions

A Read the extracts from the podcast. Underline *did* and the base form of the verbs.

Wh- questions

1 And where did this watch come from originally?

2 What did your great-grandfather use it for?

Yes/No questions

3 **A:** Did your mother take a lot of photos?
B: Yes, she did.

4 **A:** Did you buy this?
B: No, someone gave it to me.

B **WORK IT OUT** Complete the rules using words from the box. There are some words you do not need.

after before past present *wh-* questions *yes/no* questions

Simple past questions

1 We use *did* to make questions in the simple ___________.

2 Question words (*what*, *where*, *when*, *why* and *how*) come ___________ *did*.

3 We use *did/didn't* in short answers to ___________.

C **PRACTICE** Reorder the words to write simple past questions.

1 you / a special gift / did / get / on your 21st birthday
___________?

2 win / what kind of / you / did / prizes / at school
___________?

3 did / your best friend / you / meet / when
___________?

4 pass / you / did / tests / any / last year
___________?

D Go to the Grammar Hub on page XII.

E **SPEAK** Work in pairs. Ask and answer the questions in Exercise C.

PRONUNCIATION
Final consonant /t/ and /d/

10.4 **A** Read and listen to these examples. Notice the final sounds in each pair.

1 mate made
2 right ride
3 hat had

10.5 **B** Listen and choose the word you hear.

1 write / ride
2 wrote / rode
3 sent / send
4 hat / had
5 sat / sad
6 set / said

C Work in pairs. Say one word from each pair in Exercise B. Ask your partner to identify the word.

SPEAKING HUB

A **PREPARE** Work in groups. Group A – Stay on this page. Group B – Go to the Communication Hub on page XXI. Read the survey. You need to write one person's name for each sentence and find out extra information.

Find someone who:

1 … lived in another country when they were a child.
Where?

2 … passed a test not long ago.
What?

3 … wrote an email yesterday.
Why?

4 … finished college more than five years ago.
Where?

B **PLAN** Write the questions you need to ask for each item.

Did you live in another country when you were a child?
Where did you live?

C **PRACTICE** Walk around the classroom and ask questions. Write the names and the answers.

A: Did you live in another country when you were a child?
B: Yes, I did.
A: Where did you live?

D **REPORT** Work with someone from Group B. Tell them what you found out.

Elsa lived in Brazil when she was young. She lived there for three years and she loved it!

Talk about past experiences

10.3 It was amazing!

F– show interest

COMPREHENSION

A ▶ Watch the video. Who had a good weekend? Who had a bad weekend? Who had a good and bad weekend? Check (✓) the boxes.

	Good weekend	Bad weekend
 Carolina	☐	☐
 Onur	☐	☐
 Mark	☐	☐
 Gaby	☐	☐

B Answer the questions. Write the names in the spaces provided.

1 Who went to Paris? ______

2 Who watched the match? ______ ______

3 Who went to the hairdresser's? ______ ______

4 Who went to a concert? ______

5 Who had a pizza? ______

C ▶ Watch the video again and check your answers to Exercise B.

Glossary

match (n) (British) = game (n) (American)

FUNCTIONAL LANGUAGE

Showing interest

A Complete the responses to good and bad news with the words in the box.

great love nice Really shame sounds think too

Good news	Bad news
Oh, very [1] ______.	Oh no, that [7] ______ awful.
[2] ______? Wow!	Oh, what a [8] ______.
Cool. I [3] ______ Paris.	
Really? Me, [4] ______.	
Well, that's [5] ______.	
I [6] ______ it's amazing!	

B Circle the correct options (a, b or c) to complete the conversation.

Mark: Onur, what did you do?
Onur: I went to France with some friends.
Mark: Oh, [1] ______. Where did you go?
Onur: We went to Paris.
Mark: Really? [2] ______!
Onur: Yes, it was amazing.
Carolina: [3] ______, I love Paris.
Mark: And what about you, Carolina. How was your weekend?
Carolina: It was also [4] ______. I watched the match on Saturday.
Mark: [5] ______? Me too. Did you enjoy it?
Carolina: Yes, it was [6] ______.
Mark: And Gaby, what did you do this weekend?
Gaby: Well, on Saturday I went to the hairdresser's and it was bad. Then on Sunday I ate a pizza and it was bad.
Carolina: Oh no, that sounds [7] ______.
Gaby: It was.
Mark: Oh. [8] ______.

1 a very nice b bad c awful
2 a What a shame b Wow c Oh no
3 a Cool b Oh no c What a shame
4 a awful b amazing c bad
5 a Oh no b Really c That sounds awful
6 a great b awful c amazing
7 a great b awful c amazing
8 a Really b What a shame c Oh no

C ▶ Watch the video again and check your answers to Exercises A and B.

GABY

SAM

LUCY

PRONUNCIATION

10.6 **A** Listen to the conversation and notice how the <u>underlined</u> words are stressed.

Astrid: <u>What</u> did you <u>do</u> on the <u>week</u>end?
Patrick: I <u>played</u> <u>ten</u>nis. It was <u>great</u>.
Astrid: <u>That</u> sounds <u>good</u>.
Patrick: Then I had <u>lunch</u> with my <u>friend</u>.
Astrid: Oh, very <u>nice</u>.
Patrick: But the <u>food</u> was <u>ter</u>rible.
Astrid: <u>Oh</u>, what a <u>shame</u>.

10.6 **B** Listen again and repeat the conversation. Copy the stress.

SPEAKING

A PLAN Imagine you did the activities in the pictures below last weekend. Decide if they were good or bad and say why.

have a picnic

bad, rain

have brunch

amazing, delicious

go to the hairdresser's

go to a party

go to the beach

go ice-skating

B PREPARE Work in pairs. Talk about your weekends. Listen and respond to your partner.

A: On Saturday I ______________. It was ______________.
B: Oh, that sounds *great* / *good* / *bad* / *awful*!

C PRACTICE Go around the class and find out what other people did on the weekend. Listen and respond to what they say.

A: What did you do on the weekend?
B: I went to a birthday party. It was great.
A: Oh, very nice.
B: But then I watched a movie and it was bad.
A: Oh, what a shame.

Show interest

10 Writing

Write a paragraph about a past event

W – using sequencing words

A Look at the picture. What is it? Where is it from? How old is it?

B Read the story. What do you think happened next?

About | **Submit** | Contact

Every picture tells a story!
Write a story in 100 words.

A lucky coin

On Saturday morning, Jack got up early and went running in the park. After half an hour, he sat down for a break and he saw something gold under the bench. It was an old gold coin. He picked it up. Then, he put it in his pocket and went home. The next day, on his way to work, he saw a poor man and gave the gold coin to him. A few days later, Jack saw the poor man again. The man walked over to Jack and said, 'I sold the coin for $100 yesterday. Here's $50 for you.'

C Read the story and answer the questions.

1 What did Jack find? ____________________

2 Where did he find it? ____________________

3 What did he do with it? ____________________

4 What happened in the end? ____________________

Using sequencing words

Sequencing words, for example *after, then, later,* help the reader to understand the order of events in a story.

D Underline the sequencing words in the story. Put the actions in the order they happened in the story.

- ☐ Jack sat down for a break.
- ☐ Jack gave the coin to the poor man.
- ☐ Jack put the coin in his pocket.
- ☐ The poor man offered Jack money.
- ☐ Jack went running.
- ☐ Jack found a coin.

E Choose the correct options to complete the story. Finish the last line of the story.

Last week, Vicky saw a lamp in the window of an old furniture store. It was very beautiful and she looked at it for a long time. [1]*Then / After*, she went to work. A week [2]*next / later*, she came back to the store, but the lamp wasn't in the window. [3]*Later / After* a couple of minutes, she decided to …

____________________.

WRITING

A PLAN Choose one of the story starters and write notes about what happened next.

B WRITE Write the story in 100 words.

- Last summer, we were on vacation in Greece. We walked on the beach every day and one day we found …
- Yesterday morning, Julia went to a market. There were a lot of old paintings. After a few minutes, she saw …
- About three weeks ago, I found a lot of old boxes in my grandparents' garage. I opened one of them and there was …

Write a paragraph about a past event

Unit 10 Review

GRAMMAR

A Complete the sentences in the positive or negative form of the simple past.

1 She ____________ (*buy*) a new watch last Saturday. (-)

2 He ____________ (*drive*) to work on Monday. (+)

3 My father ____________ (*sell*) his car two weeks ago. (+)

4 They ____________ (*find*) the hotel last week. (-)

5 I ____________ (*wear*) a coat yesterday. (-)

6 We ____________ (*give*) her a present for her birthday. (+)

B Complete the conversation with the simple past forms of the verbs in the box.

go see take

Kit: Where [1] ____________ you ____________ last weekend?

Ben: We [2] ____________ to the art museum.

Kit: Really? What [3] ____________ you ____________ there?

Ben: We [4] ____________ some art from Ancient Greece.

Kit: Really? [5] ____________ you ____________ any photos?

Ben: Yes, I did. I [6] ____________ a lot of photos.

VOCABULARY

Complete the sentences with the simple past form of verbs from the box and the correct time expressions.

ago finish give go in (x2) last (x2) meet win

1 We ____________ to Switzerland for our vacation ____________ summer.

2 Sushila ____________ college ____________ 2014.

3 Tony ____________ first prize in the art competition two years ____________.

4 Eliana ____________ her new friend on vacation in Greece ____________ year.

5 They ____________ this watch to my father ____________ 2009.

11 HAVING FUN

Senior man with hands raised, riding a rollercoaster.

OBJECTIVES

- talk about things you like doing
- talk about favorite sports, music and movies
- make and respond to suggestions
- write a personal profile

Work with a partner. Discuss the questions.

1 Look at the picture. How do you think the man feels?

2 Do you like theme parks?

3 Read the quote. Tell each other about things you enjoy.

11.1 In or out?

Talk about things you like doing

V recreational activities G *like/love/hate/enjoy* + verb + *-ing* P verb + *-ing* /ŋ/

Is <u>STAYING IN</u> the new <u>GOING OUT</u>?

There are a lot of things you can do to relax on the weekend. You can go to a restaurant or the movie theater. Or you can go to a concert or maybe a soccer game. Did you do any of these things last weekend? For a lot of people, the answer is no. **They don't like going out.** They just want to stay at home. We talked to three people to find out why.

a

b

Why do you like staying in?

Agnes

I love movies. [1] ________________, but I don't like going to the movie theater. I don't like the food they sell there. **I love getting takeout food**, spending time with my family and watching TV and movies at home.

Lee

I'm a soccer fan, [2] ________________. You can watch games from all over the world on TV. My friends come to my house, and we chat and eat snacks, and **we enjoy watching sports together**. It's a great way to spend time with friends.

Frieda

My favorite type of music is rock. [3] ________________, and in my car. **My husband loves going to concerts** and he goes out all the time. But **I hate going to concerts** – they're expensive and there are too many people! **I like staying at home** and listening to my favorite music really loud!

READING

A SPEAK Work in pairs. Ask your partner about last weekend.

A: What did you do last weekend?
B: I went to an Italian restaurant. What about you?

B PREPARE TO READ Read the headline of *Is staying in the new going out?* and look at the pictures. Match the <u>underlined</u> words with the pictures (a and b).

C READ FOR GIST Read the first paragraph of the article. Choose the correct options to complete the summary.

There [1]***are / aren't*** a lot of things that people do to relax [2]***in the week / on the weekend***. The article says people these days mostly want to [3]***stay in / go out***.

D READ FOR DETAIL Read the rest of the article. Choose the correct phrase to fill in the blanks in the text.

a I listen to it at home
b I watch them every weekend
c but I don't go to games

E READ FOR SPECIFIC INFORMATION Read the article again and choose the correct options.

1 Agnes doesn't go to the movie theater because …
   a it's expensive.
   b she doesn't live near a movie theater.
   c she doesn't like the food.
2 Lee doesn't go to games because …
   a he can watch a lot of sports at home.
   b they're expensive.
   c he doesn't like the snacks.
3 Frieda doesn't go to concerts because …
   a it costs a lot of money.
   b she doesn't like music.
   c she doesn't like loud music.

F SPEAK Work in pairs. Are you similar to Agnes, Lee or Frieda? Give examples.

VOCABULARY

Recreational activities

A Complete the phrases with the words in the box.

~~family~~ friends a museum the park TV a video online

1 spend time with *family*

2 go to ________________

3 watch ________________

4 watch ________________

5 spend time with ________________

6 go to ________________

B Go to the **Vocabulary Hub** on **page XIX**.

C SPEAK Talk to your partner. Ask and answer questions about the recreational activities you like.

A: Do you watch a lot of TV?
B: Yes! I love it! Where do you usually spend time with your friends?
A: At a café, or sometimes at home.

GRAMMAR

like/love/hate/enjoy + verb + *-ing*

A WORK IT OUT Read the phrases in bold in *Is staying in the new going out?* Choose the correct option.

In these phrases, the people are talking about their feelings about *activities* / *objects*.

B Match the words with the emojis.

enjoy hate like love

1 ________ 2 ________ ________ 3 ________

C WORK IT OUT Complete the rules with the words in the box.

negative phrases positive phrases questions

1 In ______________, we use *like/love/hate/enjoy* + verb + *-ing*.

2 In ______________, we use *do/does* + *not* + *like/love/hate/enjoy* + verb + *-ing*.

3 In ______________, we use *do/does* + subject + *like/love/hate/enjoy* + verb + *-ing*.

D Go to the **Grammar Hub** on **page XIV**.

PRONUNCIATION

Verb + *-ing* /ŋ/

11.1 **A** Read and listen to the sentence. Choose the correct option to complete the statement.

I like listening to music in the kitchen.

The underlined letters have ***the same sound*** / ***different sounds***.

11.2 **B** Listen and repeat the sentences.

1 He likes going out and spending time with his friends.

2 She likes staying in and watching TV.

11.3 **C** Listen and circle the word you hear.

1 ban / bang 2 thin / thing 3 win / wing

11.4 **D** Listen to the questions. Write the missing words.

1 Do you like *getting* *takeout* food?

2 Do you and your friends like ________ to the same ________?

3 What do you enjoy ________ on the ________?

4 Who do you enjoy ________ ________ with on the weekend?

5 What do you hate ________ on ________?

6 Where do you like ________ out to ________?

E SPEAK Work in pairs. Ask and answer the questions in Exercise D.

A: Do you like getting takeout food?
B: No, I don't. I like going to restaurants.

SPEAKING

A PREPARE Take a class survey about free-time activities. Write three activities from the lesson and add three new activities of your own. Include some 'staying in' activities and some 'going out' activities, too.

Activity	Love	Like/Enjoy	Hate	Extra info
go to the park	✓			*near school*
watch TV				

B PRACTICE Ask other students about the activities they like, enjoy, love and hate.

A: Do you like going to the park?
B: Yes, I love it!
A: Which park do you like?
B: I like the park next to the school.

C REPORT Work in pairs. Look at your results. Answer the questions. Tell the class.

1 What activities do people like, enjoy, love and hate?

2 Do the people in the class like staying in or going out?

Ten people love going to the park. No one hates going to the park.
In general, the people in this class like going out.

Talk about things you like doing

11.2 Super fans

Talk about favorite sports, music and movies

S listening for opinions G object pronouns V entertainment P vowel sounds: /ʊ/ and /u:/

LISTENING

11.5 **A** Look at the picture below. Who is the man, and where is he from? Listen to the radio show interview and check.

11.5 **B** Listen again. Choose the correct options to complete the summary.

They are at a [1]*basketball / soccer* game in the [2]*Olympic / Athletic* Stadium between [3]*England / Germany* and Egypt.
They are waiting to [4]*play / watch* their favorite player, Mo Salah.

Listening for opinions

When we want to give our opinion about something we can use the phrase *I think* to start the sentence. We can also use adjectives, for example *interesting*, *boring*, to show how we feel about something. We use *because* to introduce reasons for our opinion.

I think he's great … I also like him because he's a nice person.

My boyfriend loves soccer, but I hate it – it's so boring.

11.5 **C** Answer the questions. Listen again and check your answers.

1 Who says Mo Salah is number one in the world? *Wendy / Kelly / Ryan*
2 Who says Mo Salah is a nice person? *Wendy / Kelly / Ryan*
3 Who says Mo Salah is good to his fans? *Wendy / Kelly / Ryan*
4 Who doesn't like any other soccer players? *Wendy / Kelly / Ryan*
5 Who isn't interested in soccer at all? *Wendy / Kelly / Ryan*

D SPEAK Work in pairs. Do you like soccer? Why/Why not?

GRAMMAR

Object pronouns

A Read these sentences from the radio show interview. Answer the questions.

Wendy: I'm here to see Mo Salah.
Interviewer: Why do you like him?

1 What or who is the object of Wendy's sentence?
2 Which word does the interviewer use to replace the object of Wendy's sentence?

B Read more sentences from the listening. Underline the object pronouns and circle the people or things they refer to.

1 Kelly: My boyfriend loves soccer, but I hate it.
2 Interviewer: What do you think about Mo Salah?
Kelly: My boyfriend likes him.
3 Interviewer: So, Ryan, what do you think about the other soccer players?
Ryan: I'm not interested in them.

C WORK IT OUT Complete the table with the object pronouns in the box.

her him it ~~me~~ them us you (x2)

Subject pronouns	Object pronouns
I play tennis with Luke.	Luke plays tennis with [1] ___me___.
You watch TV with Harry.	Harry watches TV with [2] ______.
He knows a lot of people.	A lot of people know [3] ______.
She plays soccer.	I play soccer with [4] ______.
It is a great movie.	I love watching [5] ______.
We like staying in with Mike.	Mike likes staying in with [6] ______.
You can all come to my house.	I'm happy to see [7] ______ all.
They are musicians.	I like listening to [8] ______.

D Go to the Grammar Hub on page XIV.

E SPEAK Complete the sentences with your own ideas. Then complete the questions with the correct object pronoun. Work in pairs and ask and answer the questions.

1 ______ is a famous pop singer in my country. Do you know ______?
2 ______ is the name of a stadium in my town/city. Do you know ______?
3 ______ is a sports (soccer/basketball, etc) team in my country. Do you know ______?

VOCABULARY

Entertainment

A Look at the pictures and read the sentences. Put the words in bold in the correct category.

Rihanna's one of my favorite **pop stars.** I go to all her **concerts**.

The **stadium** is always full when Brazil plays. They're really good **players** and the **games** are usually exciting.

My favorite **movie stars** were at the **movie theater** on Hollywood Boulevard to watch the **premiere**.

People:			
Events:			
Places:			

B Go to the **Vocabulary Hub** on **page XIX**.

C Choose the correct option to complete the sentences.

1 My favorite *actor* / *player* is Scarlet Johansson; I have all her movies on DVD.

2 I think Antoine Griezmann is a really good soccer *player* / *singer*.

3 Justin Timberlake was a famous *pop star* / *player* when I was a teenager.

4 There are many famous pop *players* / *stars* in my country.

5 My brother's in a *classical* / *rock* band. He plays the electric guitar.

6 I love watching *action movies* / *comedies*. All of my favorite movies are funny!

D SPEAK Work in pairs. Discuss the sentences in Exercise C. Make sentences that are true for you.

My favorite actor is …

PRONUNCIATION

Vowel sounds: /ʊ/ and /uː/

11.6 **A** Listen and repeat.

/ʊ/ took, sugar, book   /uː/ two, June, blue

11.7 **B** Listen to the sentences. Which sound do the underlined words have?

1 My father is a good cook.   /ʊ/ /uː/

2 Moon is my favorite sci-fi movie. I like horror movies, too.   /ʊ/ /uː/

11.8 **C** Listen and read the sentences. Underline the word that includes the sound in parentheses.

1 The soccer game starts soon. (/uː/)

2 I like cooking Italian food. (/ʊ/)

3 My daughter loves going to school. (/uː/)

4 I know that woman. (/ʊ/)

5 I always go out on Tuesday evening. (/uː/)

6 There are a lot of interesting things to look at in the museum. (/ʊ/)

D SPEAK Work in pairs. Make a short sentence that includes one of the words in the box. Say it to your partner. Listen and check your partner's pronunciation.

book foot good look museum the news too Tuesday

I watch the news on TV every evening.

SPEAKING HUB

A PREPARE Think about the things that you enjoy doing. Why do you like them? Write some notes.

B PLAN You are going to find out if your partner is a superfan. Write some questions. Use the words in the box to help you.

actor movies music player singer sports star

What …? Where …? Who …? Why …?

Do you like watching movies?
What movies do you like watching?
Who is your favorite actor?

C DISCUSS Work in pairs. Ask and answer the questions from Exercise B. Is your partner a superfan? Why/Why not?

Talk about favorite sports, music and movies

Café Hub

11.3 Short run

F– make and respond to suggestions

COMPREHENSION

A ▶ Watch the video. Underline the correct words or phrases. Then write *Gaby*, *Lucy* or *Both*.

1 *She* / *They* dyed *her* / *their* hair. ______
2 *She's* / *They're* free tomorrow. ______
3 *She wants* / *They want* to go to the gym. ______
4 *She likes* / *They like* breakfast a lot. ______
5 *She's* / *They're* sporty. ______
6 *She says* / *They say* they love running. ______
7 *She doesn't* / *They don't* run far. ______
8 *She has* / *They have* breakfast at Sam's Café. ______

B Correct the information in Gaby's diary. There are five mistakes.

Today	Tomorrow
Wash hair.	Meet Lucy at Newton Green at 9 am.
Call Sam.	Go swimming in the park.
	Go for breakfast at Pizza Roma.

FUNCTIONAL LANGUAGE

Making and responding to suggestions

A ▶ 00:18–01:23 Put the telephone conversation in the correct order. Then watch part of the video and check your answers.

a What about going to the gym and then we can have a big breakfast afterwards? ___
b Cool. Do you want to do something? ___
c Sure. Why don't we do something sporty? ___
d No, I'm free all day. 2
e Great, see you there. ___
f OK, how about going for a run and then breakfast? ___
g Yeah, OK. ___
h Perfect. I love running. That sounds really nice. Where do you want to meet? ___
i Er, I'm not sure about the gym, but I like breakfast a lot. ___
j Hi Lucy. Are you busy tomorrow? 1
k Let's meet at Newton Green at eight o'clock tomorrow. ___

B Complete the table with examples from the conversation in Exercise A.

Make a suggestion	Saying yes
What about + verb + *-ing* …	Sure / Great / Perfect
[1] What about going to the gym ?	That sounds [5] ______.
How about + verb + *-ing* …	**Saying no**
[2] ______?	I'm not sure about [6] ______.
Why don't we …	**Arrange a place and time**
[3] ______?	Where do you want to meet?
Let's …	Are you busy … + time/day? [7] ______?
[4] ______.	See you there.

GABY

SAM

LUCY

PRONUNCIATION

A Listen to the conversation and notice how the underlined words are stressed.
11.9

Charlie: Are you free on Saturday?
Beccie: Yes, I'm free all day.
Charlie: Cool. Do you want to do something?
Beccie: Sure. Why don't we go for a run?
Charlie Uh, I'm not sure about running.
Beccie: OK. How about going for a walk?
Charlie: Great, I love walking. Where do you want to meet?
Beccie: Let's meet at Sam's Café at nine o'clock.
Charlie: Great! See you there.

B Listen again and repeat the conversation. Copy the stress.
11.9

SPEAKING

A PLAN Work in pairs.

- Make a list of things you like doing on the weekend.
- Make a list of things you don't like doing on the weekend.

B PREPARE Practice the conversation. Then change roles.

Student A: Suggest something from the list.
Student B: Say no.
Student A: Suggest something from the list.
Student B: Say yes.

C REPEAT Go around the class and make an arrangement with five other students. Use the activities in Exercise A or your own ideas. Complete the table below.

Name	Activity	Place	Time
Sam	*Play soccer*	*The park*	*5 pm*

Make and respond to suggestions

11 Writing — Write a personal profile

W – using *so*

ABOUT ME

Sign up | Login

I'm an artist and a designer, so I love going to museums and art galleries. I have a dog; her name's Kia, and we go on a lot of walks together. I live near the ocean, so we spend a lot of time on the beach. Kia really enjoys running after the birds! I live with my husband and three sons, and they all love football. It's always on TV in our house, and I hate it. I'm not a sports fan at all, so I'm happy to go out for a walk with Kia, or to work on my art.

Helena H.

A Read the text. Join the beginnings (1–4) to the ends (a–d) to make sentences.

1	Helena is	a	going to museums and galleries.
2	She likes	b	on the beach with her dog.
3	She spends time	c	watching sports.
4	She doesn't like	d	an artist and a designer.

Using *so*

When we want to talk about a result, we can use *so*.

I'm an artist and a designer, so I love going to museums and art galleries.

I live near the ocean, so we spend a lot of time on the beach.

I'm not a sports fan at all, so I'm happy to go out for a walk.

When we write, we usually put a comma (,) before *so*.

B Use *so* to write short endings to the sentences. Use the ideas in the box to help you.

go to the gym   go shopping   go to the stadium
go to the theater   listen to music at home
spend time in the park

1 I like baseball …
2 I don't enjoy going to concerts …
3 I have three dogs …
4 I love fashion …
5 I enjoy exercise …
6 I'm a fan of Shakespeare …

WRITING

A PLAN You are going to write a personal profile. Write notes about what you like doing and why.

B WRITE Write a short personal profile for the website.

Write a personal profile

Unit 11 Review

GRAMMAR

Find and correct eight mistakes.

WHAT DO YOU LIKE DOING?

Home | Soccer | Basketball | Football | Tennis | Golf | More…

This week: Basketball star Orson Orlando

I'm a professional basketball player, but I don't like watch basketball on TV. I have three children, and I like spend time with they. We enjoying going to the park on the weekend and having fun. My wife is an actor. I love watching she but her doesn't want to watch movies on the weekend. She doesn't liking going to the movie theater, but I love its.

5h | 3

VOCABULARY

Complete the sentences with the words in the box.

actor   basketball   concert   game   premiere
restaurant   singer   takeout

1 Josh Brolin is my favorite ______________. I have all his movies on DVD.
2 I don't like cooking. I like staying in and getting ______________ food.
3 There's an international soccer ______________ on TV tonight.
4 I went to a pop concert last night but I didn't like the ______________. He wasn't very good.
5 I went to a movie ______________ and I met all the actors. It was really exciting!
6 I like sitting very close to the players when I go to a ______________ game.
7 The ______________ was very loud but I loved it!
8 I love Chinese food but I don't eat it at home. I like going to the ______________ in the town center.

12 GOING AWAY

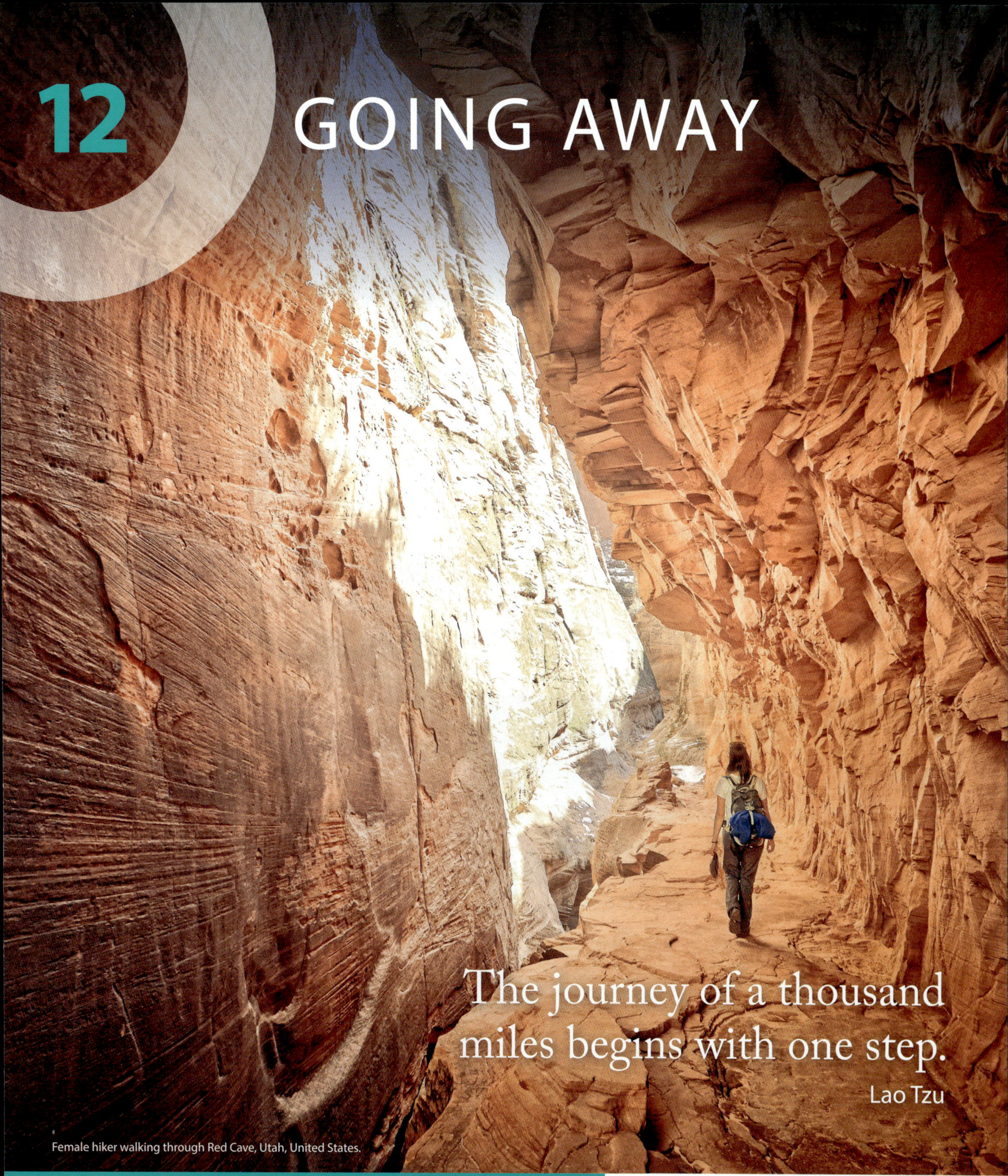

Female hiker walking through Red Cave, Utah, United States.

OBJECTIVES

- describe a trip
- talk about vacation plans
- ask for and give opinions
- write a postcard

Work with a partner. Discuss the questions.

1 Look at the picture. Do you enjoy long trips?

2 When do you usually go on vacation?

3 What makes long trips difficult?

12.1 Trips

Describe a trip

V travel P consonant clusters G countable and uncountable nouns

READING

A Work in pairs. Make a list of the problems people sometimes have when they travel.

B **READ FOR GIST** Read *A bad trip*. Choose the correct summary.

a Kate McCallister didn't take her son when she went on vacation. She tried to get home, but she had a very bad trip.

b Kate McCallister didn't take her passport when she went on vacation. She went home with her son.

C **READ FOR DETAIL** Put the events (a–e) in the order they happened (1–5). Read the article again to check your answers.

a Kate got on a plane to Paris. ___

b Kate remembered Kevin was at home. ___

c Kate went to Chicago in a van. ___

d Kate went to the airport in Chicago. ___

e Kate got on a plane to Pennsylvania. ___

D **SPEAK** Work in pairs. Answer the questions.

1 Do you ever go on a plane or a train?

2 Do you sometimes forget things when you travel?

A BAD TRIP

A lot can go wrong when you travel. For example:

- Your train to the **airport** is late, so you miss your plane.
- You take a taxi to the airport, but there is a lot of **traffic**, so you miss your plane.
- You forget your **passport**.
- Your **luggage** is too big to take on the plane.
- You forget the **bag** with all of your **money**, your **credit card** and your **ticket** in it.

These are all things that can happen, but I think the worst thing is what happened to Kate McCallister in the 1990 movie *Home Alone*. She went to Paris on vacation with her family. At first, she didn't have any problems. She got to the airport on time, she didn't forget her passport, her luggage wasn't too big, and she had all her bags and all her money with her. She also had all of her credit cards and tickets. But she forgot one very important thing.

When she was on the plane from Chicago to Paris, Kate remembered: her 8-year-old son, Kevin! Kevin was not with them. He was at home … alone!

When they got to Paris, there weren't any planes back to Chicago, so she took a plane to Pennsylvania in the United States. Then, Kate tried to get a plane from Pennsylvania to Chicago but there weren't any. So, she traveled home in a van with a traveling group of musicians. Did she get back to Kevin? Was he okay? Watch the movie to find out!

VOCABULARY

Travel

A Match the images with the words in bold in the article.

1 ______________

5 ______________

2 ______________

6 ______________

3 ______________

7 ______________

4 ______________

8 ______________

B Go to the Vocabulary Hub on page XX.

C Choose the correct options to complete the conversation.

Leo: Do you have your [1]*passport / taxi*? You need it to get on the [2]*plane / airport*.

Mia: Yes, I do. It's in my bag.

Leo: Do you have some [3]*money / luggage*? We need to exchange it at the airport for [4]*dollars / tickets*.

Mia: Yes, I do. It's in my bag.

Leo: Do you have the [5]*tickets / credit cards* for the train to the [6]*airport / station*?

Mia: Yes, I do. They're in my bag.

Leo: Do you have your bag?

Mia: Yes, I … Oh wait. No, I don't. I think it's at home.

PRONUNCIATION
Consonant clusters

12.1 **A** Listen to the sentences. Notice how we say the underlined letters.

You need your ticket to get on the <u>pl</u>ane.

I took a <u>tr</u>ain at the <u>st</u>ation.

12.2 **B** Listen to the words. <u>Underline</u> the consonant clusters.

blue class fly plane travel

12.3 **C** Listen and circle the words you hear.

1 rain / train
2 tea / tree
3 top / stop
4 red / bread
5 back / black

GRAMMAR
Countable and uncountable nouns

A Read the sentences from the article. What do you notice about the words in bold? Are they talking about one bag, or more than one?

1 You forget the **bag** that has your <u>money</u>, your credit card and your ticket in it.

2 … her luggage wasn't too big, and she had all her **bags** and all her <u>money</u> with her.

B What do you notice about the <u>underlined</u> words?

C **WORK IT OUT** Choose the correct option to complete the sentences.

Countable and uncountable nouns

1 *Bag / Money* is a countable noun: it has a singular and a plural form.

2 *Bag / Money* is an uncountable noun: it doesn't have a plural form.

D **PRACTICE** Choose the correct options. Use examples from the article *A bad trip* to help you.

1 *all of your monies / all of your money*
Money is a(n) *countable / uncountable* noun.

2 *all of her credit cards / all of her credit card*
Credit card is a(n) *countable / uncountable* noun.

3 *her luggages / her luggage*
Luggage is a(n) *countable / uncountable* noun.

4 *a lot of traffic / a lot of traffics*
Traffic is a(n) *countable / uncountable* noun.

E Go to the **Grammar Hub** on **page XVI**.

SPEAKING

A **PREPARE** Work in pairs. Read the description of a trip. Answer the questions.

I took a train from New York to Philadelphia. The train left on time but soon after we got to Pennsylvania the train stopped. There was a tree on the track and the train couldn't move! In the end, we got on a bus. We arrived in Philadelphia two hours late.

1 Where did she start?
2 Where did she finish?
3 How did she travel?
4 What was the problem?

B **PLAN** Think about a bad trip you went on. Prepare the answers to these questions.

1 Where did you start?
2 Where did you finish?
3 How did you travel?
4 What was the problem?

C **DISCUSS** Work in groups. Tell each other about your bad trips. Listen and ask questions.

And then what happened?
What did you do?
What happened next?
Oh wow, how did you …?

Describe a trip

12.2 A prize vacation

● Talk about vacation plans

S listening for feelings   V types of vacations   G present progressive   P vowel sounds: /ɪ/, /iː/ and /aɪ/

LISTENING

A SPEAK Work in pairs. Talk about your last vacation. Where did you go? What did you do?

A: I went to Lake Como in Italy. I went hiking, and I ate a lot of great Italian food.
B: For my last vacation, I didn't go away, but I didn't go to work – I just relaxed at home. It was great!

B PREPARE TO LISTEN Read the web page. Answer the questions.

Home | Listen live | Schedule   Search

HUB LIVE – ONLINE RADIO

Mikey Greene's afternoon show

In this week's competition, you can win a vacation for you and a friend.
Enter online. We will call the winner live on the radio. Listen to Tuesday's show and have your phone with you.

a

b

1 What is HUB Live?
  a a radio station
  b a TV station
  c a news website
2 Who is Mikey Greene?
  a a vacation expert
  b a singer
  c a radio presenter
3 What is the prize?
  a a radio
  b a vacation
  c a phone
4 How does a listener know they are the winner?
  a They get a phone call on Tuesday.
  b They look online.
  c They get an email on Tuesday.

12.4 **C LISTEN FOR GIST** Listen to the conversation. Choose the picture (a, b, c or d) that shows the vacation. Is the winner happy?

12.4 **D LISTEN FOR DETAIL** Listen again. Answer the questions.

1 What's the name of the competition winner?
2 What's the name of the competition winner's friend?
3 On what day of the week does the vacation start?
4 In which month does the vacation start?
5 How long is the vacation?

c

Listening for feelings

How we say things can tell the listener how we're feeling. When we're unhappy about something, we usually pause.

Jo: … No beach?

When we're angry or surprised, we usually speak loudly.

Jo: TWO WEEKS?

12.5 **E LISTEN FOR FEELINGS** Listen to Mikey and Jo. Match Jo's words (1–2) with the actions (a–b). What do they tell us about her feelings?

1 Camping. In a tent?   a loud
2 Mountains?   b pause

F SPEAK Work in pairs. Role-play the conversation when the winner tells her friend about the vacation.

A: Hi. I won a vacation for you and me.
B: That's great! Where is it?
A: Uh …

G SPEAK Work in pairs. Imagine you won this vacation. How do you feel?

d

VOCABULARY

Types of vacations

A Match two words or phrases with each of the pictures (a–d) on page 92.

a beach vacation a camping vacation a chalet the ocean a sightseeing vacation a skiing vacation a tent tourists

B Go to the **Vocabulary Hub** on **page XX**.

C ~~Cross out~~ the option that is not correct.

When you go on vacation, you can …

1 stay in a *tent* / *hotel* / *beach* / *chalet*.
2 take your *sunglasses* / *camera* / *skiing* / *snorkel*.
3 use a *guidebook* / *stove* / *sightseeing* / *camera*.

D Choose the correct option to complete the sentences.

1 We usually go *in* / *on* a beach vacation in August.
2 You can see the ocean *from* / *to* our hotel window.
3 We went sightseeing *around* / *of* Kyoto in Japan.
4 We usually go skiing *in* / *at* the mountains in January.
5 I enjoy camping *with* / *for* my friends.
6 I take a lot of photos *by* / *with* this camera.

E SPEAK Work in pairs. Discuss the questions.

1 What is your favorite type of vacation? Why?
2 How often do you go on this type of vacation?
3 What things do you take?

PRONUNCIATION

Vowel sounds: /ɪ/, /iː/ and /aɪ/

12.6 **A** Read and listen to the examples.

/ɪ/	/iː/	/aɪ/
sit	green	why
a	b	c

12.7 **B** Read and listen to the examples from the radio show. Then put the words (1–3) in the correct place in the table.

No [1]beach? Well, you're a [2]winner today. Have a great [3]time.

12.8 **C** Join the first half of the sentences (1–3) to the second half of the sentences (a–c) with underlined letters that have the same sound. Then, listen and check.

1 /ɪ/ This is
2 /aɪ/ My prize was
3 /iː/ He enjoyed

a a week at the ski resort.
b an interesting vacation.
c a guidebook.

D Choose the correct sound for each underlined word.

1 Do you like beach vacations? /ɪ/ /iː/ /aɪ/
2 Do you frequently win competitions? /ɪ/ /iː/ /aɪ/
3 Do you like Jo's prize? /ɪ/ /iː/ /aɪ/

E SPEAK Work in pairs. Ask and answer the questions in Exercise D.

GRAMMAR

Present progressive

A WORK IT OUT Read the sentences from the radio show. Choose the correct option to complete the rules.

Mikey: **You're going** … next Wednesday!

Mikey: **You're going** to the countryside, and **you're staying** in a tent, next to some mountains.

Present progressive

1 He is talking about an arrangement in the *present* / *future*.
2 He is talking about something that *is* / *isn't* fixed.

B Read the **audio script** on **page XXV**. Find six more sentences or questions when Mikey and Jo use present progressive.

C Go to the **Grammar Hub** on **page XVI**.

SPEAKING HUB

A PREPARE You are going to role-play a conversation between a radio presenter and a prize winner. Work in pairs. Choose roles.

Student A – You are the prize winner. Go to the **Communication Hub** on **page XXIII**.

Student B – You are the radio presenter. Go to the **Communication Hub** on **page XXI**.

B PRACTICE Role-play the conversation with your partner.

C DISCUSS Have a conversation with your partner. Imagine and plan a vacation you both want to go on. Think about:

- the type of vacation
- the place
- when to go
- where to stay
- how long to go for
- things to take

D REPORT Tell the class about your vacation.

We're going on a beach vacation!

Talk about vacation plans

Café Hub

12.3 Istanbul

F – ask for and give opinions

COMPREHENSION

A ▶ 00:10–00:40 Watch the first part of the video. What do you think Lucy's idea is? Choose a, b or c.

- **a** Why don't you come with me to Madrid?
- **b** Let's go on a city break!
- **c** How about going to see Metal Train tonight?

B ▶ 00:41–03:04 Watch the second part of the video and check your answer to Exercise A.

C Match Sam's comments (1–4) with the different places (a–d).

1. It's too rainy. ________
2. It's really expensive. ________
3. It's too busy. ________
4. It's really cold there right now. ________

a Copenhagen

b Helsinki

c Venice

d Dublin

D ▶ Watch the video again and check your answers to Exercise C.

E SPEAK Work in pairs. Answer the questions.

1. Which cities in the video would you like to visit?
2. Which cities in your country are like descriptions 1–4 in Exercise C?
3. Which city in the world would you most like to visit?

FUNCTIONAL LANGUAGE

Asking for and giving opinions

A Complete the phrases in the table with the words in the box.

about busy ~~going~~ Good How No really think

Ask for an opinion	Agree
What about [1] going on a city break?	That's a great/nice idea. Perfect!
What [2] ________ Dublin?	**Disagree**
[3] ________ about Istanbul?	[4] ________ way!
Give an opinion	**Agree**
I think it's [5] ________ expensive. It's really cold there right now.	Oh yeah. [7] ________ point. That's true.
It's too [6] ________ with long queues everywhere. It's too rainy.	**Disagree** I don't [8] ________ it's *that* cold/busy/rainy etc.

B ▶ Watch the video again and check your answers to Exercise A.

Glossary

city break (n) (British) = a getaway in the city (n) (American)
queues (n) (British) = lines (n) (American)

GABY

SAM

LUCY

PRONUNCIATION

A Listen to the conversation and notice how the underlined words are stressed.
12.9

Michael:	I have a cool idea. Let's go on a getaway.
David:	A weekend away? Together? But where?
Michael:	How about Paris?
David:	I think Paris is very expensive.
Michael:	Good point.-
David:	What about San Sebastián?
Michael:	No way, it's too rainy.
David:	I don't think it's that rainy!
Michael:	But, at this time of year, it rains a lot.
David:	That's true.
Michael:	OK, how about Amsterdam?
David:	Perfect!

B Listen again and repeat the conversation. Copy the stress.
12.9

SPEAKING

A PREPARE Work in pairs. List good and bad points about the cities below.

B PRACTICE Work in pairs. Write and practice a conversation using your ideas from Exercise A.

- Student A: Suggest a city for a getaway.
- Student B: Disagree with Student A three times and explain why.
- Finish the dialogue when Student B agrees with Student A.

C PRESENT Perform your conversation for the other students in the class.

D DISCUSS Find out which is the most popular city in your class.

Rome, Italy

Reykjavík, Iceland

San Francisco, US

Prague, Czech Republic

Dubai, United Arab Emirates

Ask for and give opinions

12 Writing — Write a postcard

W – editing your writing

A Read the postcard. Find:

1. the type of vacation ____________
2. the place ____________
3. a useful item ____________
4. a place to visit ____________
5. the first day of the vacation ____________
6. the last day of the vacation ____________

Hi Juan,

I'm on vacation in Casablanca. There are a lot of people, and it's very hot, but I love it! Every day, I go sightseeing. There are some great markets, and I really liked the Hassan II Mosque. It's beautiful. I have a new camera, and I'm taking a lot of photos. I got here last Thursday, and I'm going home tomorrow but I don't want to leave! See you soon.

Kyra

Editing your writing

When you write something, it's a good idea to check for any spelling, grammar or punctuation mistakes.

Im on Vaccation at paris ✗

I'm on ***vacation in*** *Paris.* ✓

B Find and correct the mistakes in this postcard text.

hi Ellie.

Im on vacation in peru. I lov it here! We went to Machu Picchu yesterday. It was beautiful? Tomorrow we going to Lake Titicaca. I can't wate!

See you when I get back,

wendy

WRITING

A PLAN Plan a postcard. Follow the instructions.

- Choose a place to write about.
- Write notes for each of the categories in Exercise A.

B WRITE Imagine you are on vacation now. Write a postcard. Use all of the information you prepared in Exercise A.

C EDIT Check your postcard for mistakes. Think about spelling, grammar and punctuation.

Write a postcard

Unit 12 Review

GRAMMAR

A Choose the correct options to complete the sentences.

1. I have some *moneys* / *money* in my bag.
2. Can I have two *ticket* / *tickets* to Buenos Aires, please?
3. I asked the staff for more *information* / *informations* about the trip.
4. My friend Anna goes on a lot of *vacation* / *vacations*.
5. I don't have any *credit card* / *credit cards*, but I have some cash.
6. Our taxi was late because there was a lot of *traffics* / *traffic*.

B Complete the conversation with the verbs in the box in the present progressive.

drive go take visit be

Sam: Where [1] ____________ you ____________ on vacation this year?

Tom: I [2] ____________ my brother in Virginia.

Sam: [3] ____________ you ____________ the train?

Tom: No, I [4] ____________. I [5] ____________ there.

VOCABULARY

Match the words with the descriptions. Use each word only once.

airport chalet guidebook passport skiing snorkel taxi tent

1. a type of vacation, usually in the mountains ____________
2. a type of transportation ____________
3. something you need when you go to another country ____________
4. a place you can stay in when you are on a skiing vacation ____________
5. something tourists use when they are sightseeing ____________
6. a place where you can get on a plane ____________
7. something you stay in when you are camping ____________
8. something you can use when you are on a beach vacation ____________

Endmatter Contents

Grammar Hub

Unit 7	VI–VII
Unit 8	VIII–IX
Unit 9	X–XI
Unit 10	XII–XIII
Unit 11	XIV–XV
Unit 12	XVI–XVII

Vocabulary Hub

7.1 Abilities	XVIII
8.2 Clothes	XVIII
11.1 Recreational activities	XIX
11.2 Entertainment	XIX
12.1 Travel	XX
12.2 Types of vacations	XX

Communication Hub

7.2 Student B	XXIII
8.1 Student B	XXII
9.2 Group B	XXII
10.2 Group B	XXI
12.2 Student A	XXIII
12.2 Student B	XXI

Audio scripts	XXIV–XXV

Grammar Hub

7.1

can / can't

	Positive	Negative
I/you/he/she/it/we/they	**I can** swim. **They can** fly.	**I can't** swim. **They can't** fly.

- We use *can/can't* when we want to talk about someone's ability or skills.

  I can run.

  I can't drive a car.

- The form of *can/can't* never changes.

  He can swim. NOT ~~He cans swim.~~

  She can't climb. NOT ~~She cans not climb.~~

	Question	Positive short answer	Negative short answer
I/you/he/she/it/we/they	**Can you** climb? **Can they** live underwater?	**Yes, I/we can.** **Yes, they can.**	**No, I/we can't.** **No, they can't.**

- We also ask *wh-* questions with *can*.

  What can you do?

  Which animals can fly?

Be careful!

- *Can* is followed by a verb without *to*.

  I can swim. NOT ~~I can to swim.~~

7.2

Possessive *'s*

Singular noun	This is **John's** sister.
Singular noun ending with -s	Is that **Chris's** brother? Is that **Chris'** brother?
Plural noun	These are the **girls'** friends.

- We use a possessive *'s* to show that something belongs to someone.

  This is Mark's bag. = This bag belongs to Mark.

- With a singular noun, we add *'s* to show something belongs to that person.

  This is the boy's dad.

- With a singular noun that ends in *-s*, we can add *'s* or *'* after the *-s*.

  This is James's sister.

  This is James' sister.

- For plural nouns that end in *-s*, we add the *'* after the *-s*.

  My cousins' house. (= I have more than one cousin and they share the same house.)

  What are your parents' names? (= You have more than one parent.)

Be careful!

- We also use *'s* as a contraction of *is* or *has*.

  His name's Bill. (= his name is)

  He's been out with his brother. (= he has)

7.1

can / can't

A Choose the correct options.

1 I can (walk) / *to walk* all day.
2 He *can't / not* speak English.
3 *Can you / You can* play chess?
4 I can swim but my brother *isn't / can't*.
5 *They can / Can they* climb with a rope?
6 **A:** Can you swim?
B: Yes I *can / swim*.
7 What things *can you / you can* do?
8 Dogs can swim but they *not / can't* fly.

B Write *can* or *can't* to complete the sentences.

1 We ______________ climb this mountain – it's not that big!
2 Fish ______________ fly.
3 My brother ______________ speak French – he's terrible at languages.
4 Sam's manager ______________ play the guitar. She's very talented.
5 She can drive a car but she ______________ ride a motorcycle.

C Complete the short answers.

1 Can you swim? Yes, ______ I can ______.
2 Can you play guitar? No, ______________.
3 Can they swim? Yes, ______________.
4 Can John speak French? Yes, ______________.
5 Can she speak Spanish? No, ______________.
6 Can fish fly? No, ______________.

D PRACTICE There is one mistake in each sentence. Correct the sentences.

1 I can to climb without ropes.
I can climb without ropes.
2 We not can jump very high.
____
3 It can flies for hundreds of kilometers.
____
4 He cans swim underwater for a long time.
____
5 Do you can dive ten meters down?
____
6 No, I don't can!
____
7 They can do play musical instruments.
____
8 We can to run very far.
____
9 She can speaks English.
____
10 Yes, I do can.
____

➤ Go back to page 50.

7.2

Possessive *'s*

A There is one mistake in each sentence. Find and correct the mistakes.

1 This is my ~~friend~~ friend's sister, Mary.
2 Sebastian is Fiona brother.
3 John's brothers names are Philip and Frederick.
4 My sisters' name is Sandra.
5 I like Davids' house.
6 Do you know Angus manager?
7 These are my parent's, Jill and Greg.
8 Where is Harry's parents house?

B Rewrite the phrases using *'s* or *'*.

1 the uncle of my friend = ______ my friend's uncle ______
2 the office of Costas = ______________
3 the names of my parents = ______________
4 the favorite restaurant of Keith = ______________
5 the daughter of my manager = ______________
6 the company of his cousins = ______________
7 the school of their sons = ______________
8 the desk of Peter = ______________

C Read the text and write *'s* or *'* in the correct places. There are six changes, including the example.

I have a busy week this week. On Monday, there's an all-day meeting in my manager's office, starting at 9 am. Then, I have to go to my son school (I have a son and a daughter) to talk to his teachers. On Tuesday, I go to Tampa for three days. We usually go in my colleague car. I always stay at a friend house in Tampa. My parents live near there, so I usually see them. My parents house is very small, so I can't stay there. Then, on Friday, we have a meeting at our company Orlando office. Finally, my vacation starts on Saturday!

➤ Go back to page 53.

Grammar Hub

8.1

Present progressive

	Positive	Negative
I	**I am talking** to my neighbor. **I'm talking** to my neighbor.	**I am not wearing** a green coat. **I'm not wearing** a green coat.
you/we/they	**We are sitting** in a café. **We're sitting** in a café.	**They are not leaving** the park. **They aren't leaving** the park. **They're not leaving** the park.
he/she/it	**It is raining** right now. **It's raining** right now.	**She is not working** at her desk. **She isn't working** at her desk. **She's not working** at her desk.

	Question	Positive short answer	Negative short answer
I	**Am I sitting** in your chair?	**Yes, you are.**	**No, you aren't. / No, you're not.**
you/we/they	**Are you drinking** coffee?	**Yes, I am.** **Yes, we are.**	**No, I'm not.** **No, we aren't. / No, we're not.**
he/she/it	**Is he taking** a selfie?	**Yes, he is.**	**No, he isn't. / No, he's not.**

- We use the present progressive to talk about things that happen now.

  I'm going to the library right now.
- We make the present progressive with the subject + *am/is/are* + verb + *-ing*.

  We're walking down the street.

  She's standing up now.
- In questions, the subject goes after *am/is/are*.

  Are you meeting your friends?
- In positive short answers, we use the subject + *am/is/are*.

  Is Malcolm watching TV right now? Yes, he is.
- In negative short answers with *you/he/she/it/we/they*, there's a choice of negative.

  Is Greg watching TV right now? No, he isn't. OR No, he's not.

Be careful!

- We cannot use the present progressive to talk about things we do every day, only for things we're doing right now.

  I'm drinking tea with my breakfast today. NOT ~~*I'm drinking tea with my breakfast every day.*~~
- We add *-ing* to the verb to make the present progressive. Some verbs have special spelling rules. For verbs that end in a consonant + *-e*, such as *have*, *come* and *make*, we cut the *-e* and add *-ing*.

  He's coming from the library. NOT ~~*He's comeing from the library.*~~
- For most verbs that end in consonant + vowel + consonant, such as *sit*, *stop* and *put*, we double the consonant and add *-ing*.

  They're stopping at the bank. NOT ~~*They're stoping at the bank.*~~

8.2

Adjective order

	Size	Age	Color
Adjectives	big short long	new old	red yellow green blue gray white
Example sentences	It's a **big red** coat. He's wearing **old green** shorts. We're wearing our **new blue** shoes.		

- We can put more than one adjective before a noun.

  I'm wearing a new red shirt.

  He has a big gray hat.
- The color adjective usually goes after the adjective for size or age.

  It's an old yellow dress. NOT ~~*It's a yellow old dress.*~~

Be careful!

- Remember to use the right article before the adjective. We use *an* in front of adjectives that start with a vowel.

  She's wearing an old blue dress. NOT ~~*She's wearing a old blue dress.*~~

8.1

Present progressive

A Choose the correct options.

1 I'm *walking* / *walk* down the street. (circled: *walking*)
2 You *are* / *is* sitting on my coat.
3 We're not *watch* / *watching* the movie now.
4 *Is she* / *She is* meeting her friend now?
5 He's *stand* / *standing* up right now.
6 They're *not looking* / *looking not* at clothes.
7 Are you *have* / *having* lunch now?
8 We're *going* / *go* to the park.

B Choose the correct answers to the questions.

1 Are you texting Darren?
 a No, you're not. **b** No, I'm not. (circled: b)
2 Is your sister having lunch?
 a Yes, she is. **b** Yes, she has.
3 Are they going to the bank?
 a No, they're not going. **b** No, they're not.
4 Am I wearing your T-shirt?
 a Yes, it is. **b** Yes, you are.
5 Is he lying down right now?
 a Yes, he's lying. **b** Yes, he is.
6 Is Harry sleeping?
 a No, he's not. **b** No, he not sleeping.
7 Are they talking to someone?
 a No, they're not talking. **b** No, they aren't.
8 Are you watching the soccer game?
 a Yes, I am. **b** Yes, I'm.

C Complete the sentences with the present progressive form of the verbs in parentheses.

1 He ___is walking___ (*walk*) to the park.
2 She ________ (*eat*) dinner now.
3 They ________ (*sit*) on a bench.
4 I ________ (*have*) a salad.
5 ________ (*you / wear*) your new coat?
6 Look! The car ________. (*not stop*)
7 ________ (*she / make*) dinner?
8 I ________ (*put*) money in the bank.

➤ Go back to page 58.

8.2

Adjective order

A Choose the correct options.

1 It's a ___ coat.
 a new red **b** red new (circled: a)
2 She has ___ shoes.
 a green old **b** old green
3 He's wearing a ___ hat.
 a big blue **b** blue big
4 Do you have a ___ dress?
 a new green **b** green new
5 I like your ___ skirt.
 a yellow long **b** long yellow
6 They don't have ___ sneakers.
 a white new **b** new white
7 It's a(n) ___ sweatshirt.
 a gray old **b** old gray
8 Michelle is wearing a ___ coat.
 a short white **b** white short

B Check (✓) the correct sentences and put an (✗) for the incorrect sentences.

1 She's wearing red long socks. ✗
2 He likes old yellow hats. ___
3 It's a gray big dress. ___
4 Those aren't new brown shoes. ___
5 They're not wearing long green skirts. ___
6 We have blue old T-shirts. ___
7 I want a big white sweatshirt. ___
8 Do you have green new shoes? ___

C Put the words in the correct order to make sentences and questions.

1 socks / brown / they're / old
 They're old brown socks.
2 has / red / coat / she / a / big
 ________.
3 wearing / green / they're / old / T-shirts
 ________.
4 you / hat / new / a / have / brown / do
 ________?
5 coat / like / I / blue / your / long
 ________.
6 a / sweatshirt / yellow / that's / big
 ________.

➤ Go back to page 61.

Grammar Hub

9.1

Simple past: *was/were*

	Positive	Negative
I/he/she/it	**It was** interesting.	**She was not** young. **She wasn't** young.
you/we/they	**You were** amazing.	**We were not** there. **We weren't** there.

	Question	Positive short answer	Negative short answer
I/he/she/it	**Was he** popular?	**Yes, he was.**	**No, he wasn't.**
you/we/they	**Were they** at home?	**Yes, they were.**	**No, they weren't.**

- The simple past forms of the verb *be* are *was, were, wasn't* and *weren't*.

  Marie Tussaud was an artist from France.

  My grandparents weren't famous.
- We use *was(n't)/were(n't)* to talk about people and things in the past.

  Nelson Mandela was the first black president of South Africa.
- For *yes/no* questions, we put *was* or *were* at the beginning of the question, followed by the subject.

  Was he a popular writer?
- For *wh-* questions, we put *what, where, why*, etc at the beginning of the question, followed by *was/were* + the subject.

  Who was that man?

  Where was it?

  Why were you late?

9.2

Simple past: regular verbs

	Positive	Negative
I/you/he/she/ it/we/they	**She lived** in Mexico. **We learned** a song.	**I did not play** tennis. **I didn't play** tennis.

- We use the simple past tense to talk about actions in the past.

  Alexander Fleming discovered penicillin in 1928.
- We form the simple past tense of regular verbs by adding *-ed* to the main verb. If the verb ends in *-e*, just add *-d*. If the verb ends in *-y*, change the *-y* to an *-i* and add *-ed*.

  start → *started*

  live → *lived*

  study → *studied*
- To form the negative, we put *did not* (*didn't*) before the main verb.

  She didn't study math.
- To talk about a period of time in the past, we can use *for* + minutes, months, years, etc.

  He lived in Spain for three years.

Be careful!

- Use *didn't* for the negative, but don't add *-d* or *-ed* to the main verb. The main verb stays the same.

  She didn't live there. NOT ~~She didn't lived there.~~

9.1

Simple past: *was/were*

A Complete the conversation with *was*, *wasn't*, *were* or *weren't*.

A: Where [1] ___*were*___ you yesterday?
B: I [2] ______________ in London.
A: Why [3] ______________ you in London?
B: We [4] ______________ at Madame Tussauds on a day trip.
A: [5] ______________ it fun?
B: Yes, it [6] ______________ amazing. There were statues of writers, actors and politicians. They [7] ______________ all so real!
A: [8] ______________ you there all day?
B: No, we [9] ______________. We [10] ______________ there for about three hours.

B Put the words in the correct order to make questions.

1 Charles Dickens / was / who ___*Who was Charles Dickens*___?
2 when / he / was / born ______________?
3 he / from London / was ______________?
4 from / where / he / was ______________?
5 rich / were / his parents ______________?
6 his best book / what / was ______________?

C Match the questions (1–6) in Exercise B and the answers (a–f).

___ **a** No, he wasn't.
___ **b** It was *Oliver Twist*, in my opinion.
___ **c** He was a famous writer.
___ **d** No, they weren't.
___ **e** He was born in 1812.
___ **f** He was from Portsmouth.

➤ Go back to page 67.

9.2

Simple past: regular verbs

A Complete the sentences with the simple past form of the verbs in parentheses.

1 Picasso ___*changed*___ (*change*) the way we look at art.
2 We ______________ (*try*) to find information about Frida Kahlo.
3 William Shakespeare ______________ (*live*) in a town called Stratford-upon-Avon.
4 Kim ______________ (*decide*) to write about Ada Lovelace for her project.
5 The women ______________ (*plant*) trees in the park.
6 I ______________ (*start*) to read a book about famous women scientists.
7 Our history class ______________ (*study*) the Anasazi people of North America last year.
8 Shelly ______________ (*remember*) to bring back my book about Wangari Maathai.

B Make the sentences negative.

1 Ada Lovelace studied art.
Ada Lovelace ___*didn't study art*___.
2 The female characters talked a lot in the book.
The female characters ______________ in the book.
3 Elena Favilli and Francesca Cavallo created a book about famous men.
Elena Favilli and Francesca Cavallo ______________.
4 Maria Sibylla Merian collected clothes.
Maria Sibylla Merian ______________.
5 Wangari Maathai planted flowers.
Wangari Maathai ______________.

C Complete the sentences with the past form of the verbs in parentheses.

1 I ______________ (*not want*) to be a dancer when I was a child.
2 We ______________ (*study*) French when we were at school.
3 My wife ______________ (*design*) the house we live in.
4 He ______________ (*start*) a new yoga class last week.
5 She ______________ (*not use*) her phone yesterday.
6 They ______________ (*not receive*) the letter last Monday.

➤ Go back to page 69.

Grammar Hub

10.1

Simple past: irregular verbs

Verb	Positive	Negative
build	**I built** a house.	**I didn't build** a house.
buy	**You bought** a good car.	**You didn't buy** a good car.
choose	**He chose** 100 objects.	**He didn't choose** 100 objects.
find	**She found** it yesterday.	**She didn't find** it yesterday.
give	**We gave** it to the teacher.	**We didn't give** it to the teacher.
go	**They went** from town to town.	**They didn't go** from town to town.
have	**I had** coffee this morning.	**I didn't have** coffee this morning.
make	**They made** tools.	**They didn't make** tools.
sell	**We sold** the house.	**We didn't sell** the house.
wear	**She wore** her new T-shirt yesterday.	**She didn't wear** her new T-shirt yesterday.

- Irregular verbs do not take *-ed* in the simple past. You have to learn each verb separately.
  They found an axe. NOT ~~*They finded an axe.*~~
  They went to the museum. NOT ~~*They goed to the museum.*~~
- In the negative, we use *didn't* + base form.
  I didn't have coffee yesterday. NOT ~~*I didn't had coffee yesterday.*~~
- In the negative, we usually use the contraction *didn't* but we can also use the long form *did not*.
  They didn't know the answer. OR *They did not know the answer.*

Be careful!

- Irregular verbs do not change form in the simple past.
  simple present: I make… / He makes… BUT *simple past: I made… / He made…*

10.2

Simple past: questions

Question	Positive short answer	Negative short answer
Did I tell you about the meeting?	**Yes, you did.**	**No, you didn't.**
Did you see the manager?	**Yes, I/we did.**	**No, I/we didn't.**
Did he win a prize?	**Yes, he did.**	**No, he didn't.**
Did she finish her work?	**Yes, she did.**	**No, she didn't.**
Did it rain yesterday?	**Yes, it did.**	**No, it didn't.**
Did we take a lot of photos?	**Yes, you/we did.**	**No, you/we didn't.**
Did they find the money?	**Yes, they did.**	**No, they didn't.**

- For *yes/no* questions, we put *did* at the beginning, followed by the subject + base form. We don't change the verb.
  Did you see that?

	Wh- questions
I/you/he/she/it/we/they	**What time did she get up**?
	How did you get to work today?
	Where did they study?
	When did he leave Jamaica?
	Why did you do that?
	Who did you talk to yesterday?

- For *wh-* questions, we put *what*, *where*, *why*, etc at the beginning of the question, followed by *did* + subject + base form.
  Where did she go?
  Who did they work with?
  What did she say?

Be careful!

- For negative answers to *yes/no* questions, we normally use the contraction.
  No, I didn't. NOT ~~*No, I did not.*~~

10.1

Simple past: irregular verbs

A Write the simple past form of the verbs.

1 have ___had___
2 make ______
3 go ______
4 build ______
5 sell ______
6 buy ______
7 give ______
8 wear ______

B Complete the sentences using the simple past form of the verbs in parentheses.

1 I ___wore___ (*wear*) a blue shirt yesterday.
2 My dad ______ (*build*) our house.
3 We ______ (*have*) coffee for breakfast.
4 Our parents ______ (*give*) us money.
5 He ______ (*buy*) a new phone.
6 They ______ (*choose*) a present for Alan.
7 My grandmother ______ (*sell*) flowers.
8 You ______ (*find*) us.

C Rewrite the sentences in Exercise B in the negative.

1 I didn't wear a blue shirt yesterday.
2 ______.
3 ______.
4 ______.
5 ______.
6 ______.
7 ______.
8 ______.

D Complete the sentences with the correct simple past form of the verbs in parentheses.

A hundred years ago, life in America was very different. They [1] ______ (*not have*) computers or cell phones. People [2] ______ (*not send*) emails. They [3] ______ (*write*) letters and [4] ______ (*send*) postcards. They [5] ______ (*not buy*) things online. They [6] ______ (*go*) to stores and markets. Stores [7] ______ (*not sell*) a lot of clothes. People [8] ______ (*make*) clothes at home. Parents [9] ______ (*give*) their children homemade toys. But even without the internet, children [10] ______ (*find*) a lot of ways to have fun by singing and playing games at home.

➤ Go back to page 74.

10.2

Simple past questions

A Match the questions (1–6) and the answers (a–f).

1 Did they watch TV last night? _d_
2 What time did you get up? ___
3 Where did you go on vacation? ___
4 Did you go to work yesterday? ___
5 How did you get to work? ___
6 Did it start on time? ___

a To Florida.
b No, it didn't.
c Yes, I did.
d No, they didn't.
e I went by bus.
f At nine o'clock.

B Complete the sentences with the words in the box.

did ~~didn't~~ we what where why

1 **A:** Did you sell him your car?
B: No, I ___didn't___.
2 **A:** ______ did you buy those clothes?
B: In town.
3 **A:** How ______ you get here?
B: By car.
4 **A:** Did you find us OK?
B: Yes, ______ did.
5 **A:** ______ did you buy that phone?
B: Because I liked it.
6 **A:** ______ time did the movie start?
B: At eight o'clock.

C Write questions in the simple past.

1 you / see / that
___Did you see that___?
2 when / you / go / to Miami
______?
3 you / build / your house
______?
4 where / you / buy / that hat
______?
5 she / wear / her new dress
______?
6 why / you / choose / that color
______?
7 they / find / the money
______?
8 what time / we / start
______?

➤ Go back to page 77.

Grammar Hub

11.1

like/love/hate/enjoy* + verb + *-ing

	Positive	Negative	Question
I/you/we/they	**I enjoy going** to the theater. **They love going** to restaurants.	**We don't enjoy staying** at home on weekends.	**Do they like spending** time with friends?
he/she/it	**He likes watching** TV. **Joanna loves playing** soccer.	**She doesn't like listening** to loud music.	**Does Frank enjoy watching** videos on his laptop?

- In positive phrases, we use *like/love/hate/enjoy* + verb + *-ing*.

  I like going to concerts.
  We love getting takeout food.
- In negative phrases, we use *don't/doesn't* + *like/love/hate/enjoy* + verb + *-ing*.

  I don't enjoy watching movies on my laptop.
  He doesn't like going to soccer games.
- In questions, we use *do/does* + subject + *like/love/hate/enjoy* + verb + *-ing*.

  Do you enjoy listening to music?
  Does Harriet like watching videos online?

Be careful!

- Make sure you put only the activity verb in the *-ing* form and not *like/love/hate/enjoy*.

  I like spending time with my friends. NOT *~~I'm liking spending time with my friends.~~*

11.2

Object pronouns

Subject pronoun	Object pronoun
I like soccer.	Sam plays soccer with **me**.
You know many people.	Many people know **you**.
He enjoys movies.	Mike watches movies with **him**.
She doesn't like TV.	Audrie doesn't watch TV with **her**.
We are musicians.	People like listening to **us**.
Do **they** play tennis?	Do Raphael and Sue play with **them**?

- We can use object pronouns to refer to object nouns.

  *The children like **Raphael**. = The children like **him**.*
  *Erin doesn't like **the videos**. = Erin doesn't like **them**.*
  *Does Helen know **Paulina**? = Does Helen know **her**?*
- Subject pronouns are *I, you, he, she, it, we* and *they*. Object pronouns are *me, you, him, her, it, us* and *them*.

  I like my teachers. My teachers like me. I like them.
  Tennis is a sport. It is fun, but Gus and Vicky don't like it.
  Leslie sings in a band. She's a good singer, and I love her.
- Object pronouns can follow *with* and *to*.

  Josh plays soccer with him.
  Do you like listening to them?

Be careful!

- Use *it* for singular object nouns, and *them* for plural object nouns.

  Mary likes that show. She watches it online. NOT *~~She watches them online.~~*
  Tom hates soccer games. He doesn't watch them. NOT *~~He doesn't watch it.~~*

11.1

like/love/hate/enjoy + verb + -ing

A Choose the correct options to complete the sentences.

1 We *enjoy* / *enjoys* going to the movie theater.
2 He *likes* / *like* watching TV shows on his laptop.
3 They *love* / *loves* spending time with family.
4 *Do* / *Does* Jenny hate going to concerts?
5 I *don't* / *doesn't* like playing tennis.
6 You *like* / *likes* seeing friends on weekends.
7 *Does* / *Do* they enjoy playing soccer?
8 He *don't* / *doesn't* like listening to music.

B Complete the sentences with the correct form of the verbs in parentheses.

1 I don't like ___doing___ (*do*) homework on weekends.
2 She loves ________ (*go*) out in her free time.
3 Do you hate ________ (*stay*) in the house all day?
4 Henry doesn't like ________ (*talk*) to his friends online.
5 They love ________ (*chat*) with people from all over the world.
6 We don't enjoy ________ (*make*) dinner at home.
7 Does Jim like ________ (*get*) takeout food?
8 I enjoy ________ (*see*) my friends on the weekend.

C Use the words in parentheses to complete the text.

My friend Lukas [1]________ (*hate / stay*) in. He's a writer and he works at home, so in the evening he [2]________ (*not like / watch*) TV. He wants to go out. Every evening! He [3]________ (*enjoy / go*) to a café or a restaurant, and he [4]________ (*love / go*) to the movie theater and the theater. I frequently go out with him, but I [5]________ (*not like / go*) out every night – it's too expensive!

➤ Go back to page 83.

11.2

Object pronouns

A Choose the correct options to complete the sentences.

1 I usually play soccer with my brother. He likes playing with ___.
(a) me b I
2 Danielle watches movies with her sister. She usually goes to the movie theater with ___.
a she b her
3 We like pop music, but we don't listen to ___ all the time.
a them b it
4 There are a lot of games at our stadium, but I don't frequently see ___.
a them b it
5 My favorite actor is Ryan Gosling. I like ___ and his movies a lot!
a him b he
6 Simon and I play tennis with my neighbor, Dina. She really enjoys playing with ___.
a her b us

B Rewrite the words in bold using object pronouns.

1 Cat videos are funny. Jill enjoys watching **cat videos**. ___them___
2 Lionel Messi is a great player. Mike and I love **Lionel Messi**! ________
3 Rihanna is a famous singer. Michelle likes listening to **Rihanna**. ________
4 Jake loves playing soccer. I don't like **soccer**. ________
5 Jan and I watch TV with my little brother. He likes spending time with **me and Jan**. ________

C Choose the correct options to complete the conversation.

Thomas: Who's a famous person in your home country, Anika?
Anika: Aishwarya Rai is a famous actress in India. Do you know [1]*it* / *her*?
Thomas: Yes, I think so. She's famous in the US, too. Do you enjoy watching her movies?
Anika: Yes, I do. I frequently watch [2]*her* / *them*. Who's your favorite actress or actor?
Thomas: I really like Benedict Cumberbatch. He's great in the TV show *Sherlock*. I enjoy seeing [3]*him* / *he* as Sherlock Holmes.
Anika: Yes, he's very good. *Sherlock* is a good show, but I don't watch [4]*it* / *him* regularly.
Thomas: And what about sports? Do you like [5]*them* / *us*, too?
Anika: I love tennis. My favorite player is Serena Williams. [6]*Her* / *She* is amazing!
Thomas: Yes, she is. My friend Paul and I watch tennis all the time, too. Would you like to watch tennis with [7]*her* / *us* some time?
Anika: That sounds great, thanks! I know your friend Paul. I sometimes see [8]*it* / *him* at college.

➤ Go back to page 85.

Grammar Hub

12.1

Countable and uncountable nouns

Countable nouns	Uncountable nouns
bag/bags	**cash**
card/cards	**information**
dollar/dollars	**luggage**
hour/hours	**money**
ticket/tickets	**traffic**
train/trains	**water**

- A countable noun is a noun we can count – we can have one, two or more.

  one passport *two passports*
  I don't have a passport.
  My friend has two passports – he's American and Italian.
- We can't count uncountable nouns.

  water NOT ~~one water, two waters~~
  What's happened? There's water all over the floor!
- We use a singular verb with uncountable nouns.

  Money is … NOT ~~Money are …~~
  I think money is very important.
  Money isn't important. It's more important to be happy!
- We never use *a* or *an* with uncountable nouns.

  Money … OR The money … OR Some money … NOT ~~A money …~~
  The money for the taxi is on the table.

Be careful!

- Never make an uncountable noun plural. Uncountable nouns do not have plural forms.

  information NOT ~~informations~~

12.2

Present progressive

	Positive	Negative	Question
Present progressive	**I'm taking** my camera with me.	**They aren't staying** in a hotel.	**Is Tina going** skiing?

- You know that we use the present progressive to talk about things happening now (see Unit 8). We can also use the present progressive to talk about the future. In this sentence, the people aren't traveling right now – the trip is in the future.

  We're traveling to France next week.
- We use the present progressive like this to talk about our plans for the future.

  Helga is staying in a hotel. (She booked it last week.)
  The girls are flying to the US. (They have their tickets and passports.)
- We frequently use future time expressions with the present progressive when we are talking about future plans:
  e.g. *tomorrow, next week, soon, in the summer, this evening*.

Be careful!

- You can only use the present progressive for the future if there's a plan.

  I'm watching a soccer game tomorrow. NOT ~~I'm winning a soccer game tomorrow.~~

12.1

Countable and uncountable nouns

A Complete the table with words from the box to make pairs of countable and uncountable nouns.

credit cards homework hours luggage music sandwiches ~~traffic~~ water

Countable nouns	Uncountable nouns
cars	1 *traffic*
bags	2
3	money
songs	4
exercises	5
6	food
7	time
bottles	8

B Choose the correct options to complete the sentences.

1 Australian passports *is* / *are* blue.
2 These exercises *is* / *are* really difficult!
3 The traffic *was* / *were* bad today.
4 The sun *is* / *are* too hot today!
5 The taxi *was* / *were* late and we missed our flight!
6 The cash *isn't* / *aren't* here!
7 The music *was* / *were* great at the party!
8 The food *is* / *are* on the table.

C If the phrase in bold is correct, put a check mark (✓). If it's wrong, put an (✗).

1 I want **an information** about train times, please. *✗*
2 We made **a plan** to meet tomorrow. ___
3 Do you like **a music**? ___
4 I don't have **a credit card**. ___
5 Do you want **a sandwich**? ___
6 Do you want **a food**? ___
7 Here's **a bag** for the plane. ___
8 Do you have **a luggage** for the plane? ___

D Complete the sentences with the words in the box and choose C (countable noun) or U (uncountable noun).

cash dollars information plane ticket

1 We took a ______________ from Madrid in Spain to Bogotá in Colombia. *C / U*
2 I changed my euros into ______________ at the airport. *C / U*
3 I asked for some ______________ about the trip at the train station. *C / U*
4 I need some ______________. Some stores don't take credit cards. *C / U*
5 I got a(n) ______________ for the train to Ankara. *C / U*

➤ Go back to page 91.

12.2

Present progressive

A Are these sentences about what's happening now or a plan in the future? Choose (N) for Now or (P) for Plan.

1 Ssh! The children are doing their homework. *N / P*
2 We're flying to Paris next week. *N / P*
3 I'm staying in a tent and it's cold! *N / P*
4 We're meeting at the train station. Don't be late! *N / P*
5 Gemma is waiting to get on her flight. She's bored. *N / P*
6 What time are we meeting Lauren? *N / P*

B Complete the conversation using the present progressive. Use the words in parentheses to help you.

Axel: What 1 ______________ (*you / do*) this summer?
Ben: 2 ______________ (*I / go*) on a sightseeing vacation in Istanbul.
Axel: Great! Who 3 ______________ (*you / go*) with?
Ben: 4 ______________ (*I / go*) with my sister. She's a photographer.
Axel: 5 ______________ (*she / take*) her camera?
Ben: No, 6 ______________ (*she / be*). She doesn't like working when she's on vacation.

C Complete the sentences and questions with the correct present progressive form of the verbs in parentheses.

1 *Are you traveling* (*you/travel*) by train or by bus?
2 My parents ______________ (*not/take*) a lot of luggage with them.
3 Alexander ______________ (*go*) skiing next week.
4 Where ______________ (*you/stay*)?
5 The students ______________ (*go*) sightseeing around Kyoto tomorrow.
6 We ______________ (*camp*) in the mountains for the summer.
7 What ______________ (*Ali/take*) with him on vacation?
8 Sara ______________ (*not/work*) next week.

➤ Go back to page 93.

7.1 Abilities

Look at the pictures. Use the verbs *make*, *play*, *ride* and *speak* to make phrases about abilities.

make play ride speak

1 ___*ride*___ a bicycle
2 ____________ a cake
3 ____________ Chinese
4 ____________ an omelette

5 ____________ Spanish
6 ____________ tennis
7 ____________ the piano
8 ____________ a horse

➤ Go back to page 51.

8.2 Clothes

Match the words in the box with the pictures.

cap coat dress hat jacket jeans pants shirt shoes skirt suit sweater

1 ____________
2 ____________
3 ____________
4 ____________

5 ____________
6 ____________
7 ____________
8 ____________

9 ____________
10 ____________
11 ____________
12 ____________

➤ Go back to page 60.

11.1 Recreational activities

Complete the table with the recreational activities in the box.

get takeout food · go to a concert · go to a soccer game · go to a restaurant · ~~listen to music~~ · watch soccer on TV

Going out	Staying in	Both
		listen to music

➤ Go back to page 82.

11.2 Entertainment

Match the words in the box with the pictures.

~~action~~ · baseball · basketball · classical · comedy · horror · jazz · pop · rock · sci-fi · soccer · tennis

Types of music

1 ____________

2 ____________

3 ____________

4 ____________

Types of sports

1 ____________

2 ____________

3 ____________

4 ____________

Types of movies

1 *action*

2 ____________

3 ____________

4 ____________

➤ Go back to page 85.

Vocabulary Hub

12.1 Travel

Match the phrases to the pictures.

by bike | by bus | by car | by plane | by taxi | by train | by trolley | on foot

a ______

b ______

c ______

d ______

e ______

f ______

g ______

h ______

➤ Go back to page 90.

12.2 Types of vacations

A Match the words with the pictures.

a camera | a guidebook | skiing goggles | skis | a snorkel | a stove | sunglasses | a tent

a ______

b ______

c ______

d ______

e ______

f ______

g ______

h ______

B Choose two things from Exercise A that you use when you go on …

- a beach vacation: ______, ______
- a camping vacation: ______, ______
- a sightseeing vacation: ______, ______
- a skiing vacation: ______, ______

➤ Go back to page 93.

10.2

Group B

A PREPARE Read the survey. You need to write one person's name for each sentence and find out extra information.

B PLAN Write the questions you need to ask for each item.

Did you win a prize or a competition at school?
What kind of competition did you win?

Find someone who:

1 ... wanted to be a doctor when they were a child
Why?

2 ... won a prize or a competition at school.
What?

3 ... collected something when they were young.
What?

4 ... had a favorite toy when they were a child.
What?

C PRACTICE Walk around the classroom and ask questions. Write the names and the answers.

A: Did you want to be a doctor when you were a child?
B: Yes, I did.
A: Why did you want to be a doctor?

D REPORT Work with someone from Group A. Tell them what you found out.

Paolo won an art competition when he was at school. He won first prize.

➤ Go back to page 77.

12.2

Student B

You are the presenter of a radio show. You are going to call your partner and tell them they are the winner of a vacation. Write notes about what to say:

Vacation type: skiing

Place: mountains, Switzerland

Start: next Thursday

How long: ten days

Hello, is that ...?
Congratulations! You are the winner.

➤ Go back to page 93.

Communication Hub

9.2

Group B

A PREPARE Complete the sentences with the past tense of the verbs in the box. Then choose the correct information (a, b or c) to complete the sentences.

design receive travel walk

1 Ibn Battuta ________________ from Morocco to China in the …
   a 10th century. b 12th century. c 14th century.
2 Gabriel García Márquez ________________ the Nobel Prize in Literature in …
   a 1972. b 1982. c 1992.
3 Neil Armstrong ________________ on the moon in …
   a 1959. b 1969. c 1979.
4 Steve Jobs and Steve Wozniak ________________ the first personal computers in …
   a 1966. b 1976. c 1986.

B PRACTICE Read your sentences to Group A. They will check your answers.

C PRACTICE Listen to Group A's sentences. Check their answers.

Correct sentences:

1 Larry Page and Sergey Brin **started** the company Google in **1998**.
2 John Couch Adams **discovered** the planet Neptune in **1846**.
3 William Shakespeare **lived** in England in the **16th century**.
4 Malala Yousafzai **received** the Nobel Peace Prize in **2014**.

➤ Go back to page 69.

8.1

Student B

Look at the instructions below.

- Look at the picture.
- Describe the people and what they are doing to your partner.
- Listen to your partner's description of their picture.
- Find six differences.

➤ Go back to page 59.

12.2

Student A

You are the listener of a radio show. You entered a competition on the radio show's website to win a vacation. Read the information below, then answer your phone and talk to the radio presenter.

- You don't like cold weather.
- You don't have a passport.
- You're a doctor. You're working at the hospital next week.

➤ Go back to page 93.

7.2

Student B

B PREPARE Read the information about this person. Write questions to find the missing information.

UTA ABE and her brother Hifumi are from Japan. Hifumi is very good at [1] ______________ and is a world champion. Uta is good at [2] ______________. She's the 2017 Junior World Champion. Hifumi and Uta are the winners of [3] ______________.

1 What is Hifumi good at?
2 What ...?
3 What ...?

C DISCUSS Now ask your partner questions to complete the missing information. Answer your partner's questions.

D REPEAT Repeat with the information below.

ALISTAIR BROWNLEE is from [1] ______________. He is good at triathlons – three events in one race. He can [2] ______________ – and he's fast! His brother is good at triathlons, too. His brother's name is [3] ______________. They both have Olympic medals.

➤ Go back to page 53.

Audio scripts

Unit 7

Lesson 7.2 Listening, Exercise B

7.2 **O = Oliver C = Carrie**

O: Welcome to *The People Show*. Today's special person is a very interesting young musician. His name's Sheku Kanneh-Mason and he's from Nottingham in the UK. Tell us more, Carrie.

C: Hi, Oliver. Sheku Kanneh-Mason's an amazing musician. He's the winner of the 2016 BBC Young Musician of the Year Award, and he was a musician at Prince Harry and Meghan Markle's wedding in May 2018.

O: What instrument does he play?

C: He plays the cello. But Sheku isn't the only musician in his family. He has six brothers and sisters, and they're all wonderful musicians.

O: Six? Wow! So, there are seven children in the Kanneh-Mason family?

C: That's right. Braimah is Sheku's brother. He plays the violin. Isata is Sheku's sister, and she plays the piano. They are all students at London's Royal Academy of Music. Sheku also has four younger sisters.

O: What instruments do they play?

C: Konya and Aminata play the violin, and Jeneba and Mariatu play the cello. These four can all also play the piano.

O: Are they students at the Royal Academy of Music, as well?

C: No, they don't go there – not yet anyway. They're too young right now.

O: So, is everyone in the Kanneh-Mason family a musician?

C: No, they aren't. Sheku's parents' names are Kadiatu and Stuart. They don't play any musical instruments.

O: I'm not surprised. It's difficult to find the time to play an instrument when you have seven children!

Unit 8

Lesson 8.1 Listening, Exercise C

8.1 **A = Officer A B = Officer B**

A: Can you see the man?

B: Yes. I'm watching him now.

A: What's he doing?

B: He's having lunch.

A: Is he talking to anyone?

B: No, he isn't. He's by himself.

A: Is he in a café?

B: No, he's sitting on a bench. He's eating a sandwich and drinking coffee.

B: OK … he's finishing his lunch.

A: Where's he going now?

B: He's stopping at the bank.

A: The bank! OK. This is it.

B: Wait. He isn't going to the bank. He's looking at his phone. I think he's reading a message. OK. He's walking. He's going to … the library.

A: The library? OK. Stay with him.

B: He's in the library.

A: Right. What's he doing there?

B: He's talking to someone. She's showing him something.

A: What is it?

B: It's …

A: Yes?

B: It's a book!

A: A book. What's happening now?

B: He's leaving.

A: Stay with him.

B: I can see him.

A: What's he doing?

B: He's going to the bank.

A: The bank! OK. This time … This is it.

B: Wait. He's not going to the bank. He's going to the park.

A: The park? Is he meeting anyone?

B: No, he isn't.

A: Argh. What's he doing?

B: He's lying down. He's taking a nap. I think he's sleeping.

A: What? Are you watching the right man?

B: Yes, I am! He's tall, he has gray hair and he's wearing a green coat.

A: No, that's not him. Our man has a gray coat, not a green coat. You're watching the wrong man. What's that noise?

B: Um … It's coming from the bank.

Unit 9

Lesson 9.1 Listening Exercise B

9.1 **A = Anna Ni = Nick AG = Audio Guide**

A: Oh, who's this? Was she a model?

Ni: Oh, I don't know. Push the button. Let's find out who she was.

AG: Meet Hollywood actor Audrey Hepburn. She was born in Belgium on May 4, 1929. Her movies were very popular in the 1950s and 60s. She wasn't just an actor, she was also a dancer and a model. She was famous for her beautiful clothes!

A: Hey Nick, come here. Look! Why was he famous?

Ni: I don't know. Let's listen.

AG: William Shakespeare was born in Stratford-upon-Avon in England on April 26, 1564. He was a famous writer. He's famous for plays such as Romeo and Juliet, and Hamlet. He wasn't just a writer, he was an actor, too. His plays were very important for the English language. Hundreds of the words we use in English today come from Shakespeare.

Ni: Look over here. I don't know who this is. Do you know?

A: No idea!

AG: Marie Tussaud was born in Strasbourg in France on December 1, 1761. She's now famous for the Madame Tussauds museum in London. Marie Tussaud was very good at making wax models of people and her waxworks were very popular. Photographs weren't common at the time, but Marie Tussaud made a waxwork of herself – was this a type of selfie?

A: That was really interesting! Now, we know who this is! He was President of …

Ni: South Africa!

AG: This famous politician was born in South Africa on July 18, 1918. His name is Nelson Mandela. He was in prison for 27 years. Later, he was president for five years from 1994 to 1999. He was the first black president of South Africa.

Unit 10

Lesson 10.2 Listening, Exercise B

10.3 **P = Presenter J = Janine A = Alfie I = Isabel**

P: In today's podcast, we invited three people to tell us about a family object that has a special meaning for them. Janine, hi and welcome to our podcast. Please tell us about the family object you brought with you today and why it's important to you.

J: Hi! Yes, this silver pocket watch belonged to my great-grandfather. He gave it to his son, and his son gave it to my father – and my father gave it to me when I finished college.

P: So it has a lot of family history. Where did this watch come from? What did your great-grandfather use it for?

J: I think he bought it in the 1880s from a famous watchmaker in New York. He worked on the railroads, and he used this watch every day. He made sure the trains were on time. So that's why this watch reminds me never to be late!

P: That's an amazing story. Thank you! Now, let's talk to Alfie. That looks like a nice camera, Alfie.

A: Thanks. My mother gave it to me. She bought it in the 1970s.

P: It was probably very modern in those days! Did your mother take a lot of photos?

A: Yes, she did. She took a lot of photos of me and my brother when we were young. She gave me the camera on my 16th birthday. That's probably why I became a photographer.

P: That's so interesting. And finally, let's talk to Isabel. This is a beautiful necklace. Did you buy this or did someone give it to you?

I: Actually, these pearls belonged to my grandmother. My grandfather gave them to her on the day they got married. Then, she gave me this necklace when I got married. I loved my grandmother very much. I always think of her when I wear this necklace. That's why the necklace is so important to me.

P: That's wonderful! Thanks so much to all of you for sharing your stories with us today. I'm afraid that's all we have time for today, but don't forget if you have stories to share, upload your photo and a brief description on our website!

Unit 11

Lesson 11.2 Listening, Exercise A

11.5 I = Interviewer W = Wendy K = Kelly R = Ryan

I: This is the *Sports Talk* soccer show and I'm at the Olympic Stadium in Berlin for this international friendly game between Germany and Egypt … and as you can hear, there are a lot of people here. They come from all over the world, and many of them are here to see one man: Mo Salah, the soccer superstar from Egypt. Hi! Can I ask you a few questions?

W: Sure. No problem.

I: What's your name?

W: I'm Wendy.

I: Who are you here to see, Wendy?

W: Mo Salah – I'm such a big fan!

I: Why do you like him?

W: I think he's great. I love watching him play. I also like him because he's a nice person. He's always good to his fans.

I: Thanks, Wendy. Hi, can I ask you a few questions?

K: Um … OK.

I: What's your name?

K: Kelly.

I: OK Kelly, what do you think about Mo Salah?

K: Um … My boyfriend likes him. I don't know.

I: Are you a soccer fan?

K: No, I'm not. My boyfriend loves soccer, but I hate it – it's so boring.

I: Oh … OK, well, um … is this your boyfriend?

K: Yeah, that's him.

I: Hello, can I ask you …

R: He's Egyptian and he's amazing and Mohammed's his name.

I: OK, great. So, what's your name?

R: Ryan.

I: So, why are you …

R: Mo Sa-la-la-la-lah! Mo Sa-la-la-la-lah!

I: Why are you a big Mo Salah fan, Ryan?

R: Because he is the number one in the world!

I: Do you watch Mo Salah play a lot?

R: I watch every game he plays – club and country.

I: So, Ryan, what do you think about the other soccer players?

R: I'm not interested in them. I only like Salah!

I: Thanks, Ryan. I hope you enjoy watching the game. Well, the game starts in one hour.

Unit 12

Lesson 12.2 Listening, Exercise C

12.4 M = Mikey Greene J = Jo

M: Now listeners, it's three o'clock on Tuesday afternoon and it's time to call this week's competition winner. Have your phone with you – we are calling … now!

J: Hello?

M: Is this Jo?

J: Yes, yes, yes! Is this Mikey?

M: It's Mikey Greene and you're on the radio! Congratulations, Jo – you are this week's competition winner!

J: Wow! That's amazing. I never win anything.

M: Well, you're a winner today.

J: I can't believe it. Me?

M: That's right, Jo. Your prize is a vacation for you and a friend.

J: Wow! I don't usually enter competitions, but I saw the picture on the website of the beach and the ocean, and I thought, 'This is the vacation for me!' I'm so excited.

M: The picture on the website? Oh, right, yeah. Um … that's not a picture of the vacation you're going on.

J: Oh, really?

M: Yes, you're going on a different kind of vacation. But don't worry. It's an amazing vacation.

J: Oh. OK then.

M: Who are you taking with you?

J: I'm taking my friend, Charlotte. She loves going to the beach.

M: That's great, Jo, but just to be clear: you're not going on a beach vacation this time.

J: No beach?

M: Um … no.

J: What kind of vacation is it, Mikey?

M: Well, Jo … it's a camping vacation!

J: Camping. In a tent?

M: That's right. You're going to the countryside, and you're staying in a tent, next to some mountains.

J: Mountains? Charlotte hates walking and she doesn't like cold weather. When are we going?

M: You're going … next Wednesday!

J: Next Wednesday? It's November, Mikey. It's really cold. How long are we going for?

M: It's a two-week vacation, Jo. Isn't that great?

J: Two weeks? In a tent? In the cold?

M: Next to a mountain. That's right, Jo. Have a great time. Bye, Jo. Well listeners, I think Jo's really excited about her vacation. Next week's competition is … a beach vacation in Brazil.

Notes

Macmillan Education
4 Crinan Street
London N1 9XW
A division of Macmillan Education Limited

Companies and representatives throughout the world

American Language Hub Starter B Student's Book ISBN 978-1-380-04677-2
American Language Hub Starter B Student's Book with Student's App
ISBN 978-1-380-04671-0

Written by Ingrid Wisniewska and Ed Price

First published 2020

Designed by emc design ltd
Illustrated by Daniel Límon (Beehive Illustration) pp58, 59, 60, 63, 70, 92, XVIII, XIX, XXII.
Cover design by Restless
Cover photograph by Getty Images/Valentinrussanov
Picture research by Emily Taylor
Café Hub videos produced by Creative Listening.
Café Hub video scripts written by James and Luke Vyner.

Authors' acknowledgements
Ingrid Wisniewska would like to thank her husband Greg for his constant support and encouragement.

Ed Price would like to give special thanks, always, to Becca and Henry.

The authors and publishers would like to thank the following for permission to reproduce their photographs:

Alamy pXX(12.1.a), Aflo Co. Ltd p53(tr), Aurora Photos p50(c), Pat Canova p76(L_c), Lev Dolgachov p68(1), Vadym Drobot p61(a), Endless Travel p66(Tussaud), Rostislav Glinsky pXX(12.1.b), Granger Historical Picture Archive p72(tml), Heritage Image Partnership Ltd p74(b), imageBROKER pp50(a), 51(2), Interfoto p67, Kamila Koziol pXX(12.2.e), Dennis MacDonald p72(tmr), Mauritius Images p66(Shakespeare), Peter Mayer pXVIII(8.2.2), Photopat p90(7), The Picture Art Collection p75(tl), Alan Schein p90(4), Sho Tamura/Aflo Sport pXXIII(t), Tetra Images p82(Agnes), Visuals Stock p76(V_b); **Artifacts Images** p90(3); **Blend Images**/Steve Smith pXVIII(8.2.9); **Corbis** pp96(tl), XX(12.2.h); **Decisive Images** pXVIII(8.2.4); **Getty Images** pp61(SH_b, bl), 62–63(background), 66(background), 70–71(background), 78(bl), 82(a), 82(Lee, Frieda), 90(2), 95(br), XVIII(7.1.6, 7.1.8), XIX(cml), XX(12.2.a), AFP p72(tr), 10'000 Hours pp83(br), XXI(tr), Dmytro Aksonov p64(a), Anadolu Agency p66(Hepburn), Subodh Agnihotri p94(b), Ann Ronan Picture Library/Heritage Images p74(l), Thomas Barwick p51(4), Alistair Berg p82(2), Margarita Almpanezou p94(a), Nick Ballon pXIX(bml), Blend Images/Dmitry Ageev pXVIII(8.2.6), Blend Images/KidStock p82(1), Blend Images/Patrick Lienin p92(c), Biddiboo p77, Brand X p59(8), Caiaimage p79(party), Helen Cathcart p61(SH_a), Cavan Images p76(V_c), Petar Chernaev p59(1), Razvan Ciuca p73, Corbis p61(b), Derek Croucher pXX(12.1.e), Cultura RF pp50(b), 70(tl), 79(hairdresser) 82(3,4), XVIII(7.1.1), Nick David p51(f), DigitalVision pXVIII(7.1.3), XIX(tml), DigitalVision/ Punchstock p68(7), Dougal Waters Photography Ltd p88, E+ p82(b), Eclipse_images p59(7), EyeEm pXX(12.2.c), EyeEm/Marco Agnoletti pp86–87(background), EyeEm/Pinghung Chen p71(br), EyeEm/Urs Flueeler pp54–55(background), EyeEm/Bill Green p94(d), EyeEm/Bruno Guerreiro pp94–95(background), EyeEm /Nathan Motoyama p71(tl), EyeEm/Classen Rafael p51(a), EyeEm/Tori Seubert p51(5), EyeEm/Artem Varnitsin p 59(4), FilmMagic p85(tl), Filmstudio p51(c), fStop p90(1), Charley Gallay/Stringer p85(bl), David Clapp Photography pXIX(bmr), Eleonora Galli p79(beach), Steve Glass p61(d), Kodiak Greenwood pXX(12.1.g), Jorg Greuel p95(bl), Hero Images pp59(2), 69, Heimsmyndir/Stígur Már Karlsson p68(tr), Chris Hepburn p95(tl), Justin Horrocks p76(V_d), Icon Sport p85(cr), The Image Bank pXVIII(8.2.11), Image Source pp64(br) XVIII(7.1.2, 7.1.7, 8.2.8), iStockphoto pp71(bl), 80, 90(5,6), 92(b,d), 92–93(background), 96(tr), XVIII(7.1.5, 8.2.7), XIX(tl), Johner RF p79(picnic), Julian Elliott Photography p95(tr), Letizia Le Fur pXVIII(8.2.1), Warren Little p53(br), Lonely Planet Images p96(bl), Glenn Losack p65, Maskot pp68(5,6), 82(5), Chris McKay pXIX(tmr), Donald Miralle pXXIII(b), MoMo Productions p51(e), Mondenkind p83(emojis), Kelvin Murray pp68(3), 75(b), NurPhoto p84(b), OJO Images p51(b), James O'Neil p89, onfilm pXX(12.1.d), Cecilia Pensini pXVIII(8.2.3), PeopleImages pp51(3), 76(br), 79(tr), Perspectives p61(SH_c), Photolibrary pXVIII(7.1.4), Photononstop p90(8), Marc Romanelli p93(br), RooM RF pp94(c), XVIII(8.2.5), XX(12.2.b), RonTech2000 p71(tr), Clive Rose p84(inset), Science Photo Library RF pXIX(br), Sequya p54(image on book), Jordan Siemens pXX(12.1.h), Silent Resilience Photography p68(2), skynesher pXIX(cml), SolStock p62(b), Alexander Spatari p79(brunch), Dave Stamboulis p71(mr), Stone Sub pp59(5), 81, XIX(bl), Harald Sund pp78–79(background), Taxi p82(6), Ron Thomas p95(cm), Nicola Tree p51(1), UIG p74(r), Jodie Wallis pXXI(b), Westend61 pp51(6,d), 61(c), 79(skating), XVIII(8.2.10), XIX(cr), Westend61/Jo Kirchherr pXX(12.2.d), Wireimage/Sarahphotogirl p49, Peter Zelei p68(4); **Hero Images** pp64(b), 76(V_a); **LWA**/Dann Tardif p68(8); **iStockphoto** pp71(ml), Wandersmann/Getty Images pXX(12.1.f); **Monkeybusinessimages** pXIX(cl); **People Images** pXVIII(8.2.12); **Photodisc** Bruce Leighty ppXX(12.1.c), pXX(12.2.f); **PlainPicture**/Steven Kazlowski p57; **Shutterstock**/20th Century Fox/Kobal/REX pp90–91(b), Grisha Bruev p76(L_a), Hauke-Christian Dittrich/EPA/REX p66(Mandela), Imagine China/ REX p74(t), Guy Levy/BAFTA/REX p52, Mars0hod p96(br), Monkey Business/ REX p59(6), Volis61 p76(L_b), Roman Voloshyn pXIX(tr); **Superstock** pp72(tl), 92(tl, a); **Thinkstock** ppXX(12.2.g); **Westend61**/Marco Govel p59(3).

Commissioned photographs by Creative Listening pp54, 55, 62, 63, 71, 78, 79, 86, 87, 94 and 95.

Printed and bound in Mexico
Compañía Editorial Ultra, S.A. de C.V.

2021 2020

4 3 2 1